Health and Wellbeing
SPHE 1

Anne Potts

Nodlaig O'Grady

The Educational Company of Ireland

Edco

The paper used in this book comes from Managed Forests in Northern Europe. For every tree felled, at least one new tree is planted

First published 2017
The Educational Company of Ireland
Ballymount Road
Walkinstown
Dublin 12

www.edco.ie

A member of the Smurfit Kappa Group plc

ISBN: 978-1-84536-720-6

Book design: Design Image
Cover design: Graftrónaic
Layout: Graftrónaic
Editor: Aoife Barrett
Proofreader: Sally Vince
Photographs: Shutterstock.com; iStock.com
Illustrations: Simon Smith (Beehive Illustration); Food Pyramid (p. 59) reproduced courtesy of the Department of Health, Public Sector Information (http://health.gov.ie); Eatwell Guide (p. 60) reproduced courtesy of Public Health England, licensed under the Open Government Licence v3.0 (www.gov.uk/government/publications/the-eatwell-guide); Kim Shaw; Igloo Animations; Shutterstock.com; iStock.com

05M20

Contents

Introduction

Welcome to *Health and Wellbeing: SPHE 1*. We hope you enjoy working through the first year of a three-year programme that is designed to help you to become (or remain!) a confident, happy, healthy and connected young person.

The aims of the health and wellbeing Social Personal and Health Education (SPHE) classes are to give you the space to:

- Learn about yourself
- Care for yourself and others
- Make informed decisions about your health and wellbeing.

Health and Wellbeing: SPHE 1 is designed to involve you in your own learning, by using theory and activities that make you think about the topics, give you the opportunity to discuss these issues and to apply what you have learned to your own life. You will also find follow-up references listed: websites, videos and help agencies. To help make your learning in SPHE stimulating, this book is full of interesting information and activities such as drama, collage, quizzes, animations, debates, film making, cartoons and PowerPoint and oral presentations.

To help you get the most out of SPHE we have used language that is easy to understand. At the beginning of each unit you will find the **Learning Outcomes** for that Unit, which you can tick off as you achieve them. There is also a list of **Key Words** for the Unit which are explained in clear, simple terms throughout the text, **Did You Know?** boxes with fun facts, and research findings and background information on the topics.

To help you keep track of your learning there are **Learning Logs, Assessment: Check your learning** activities and **Unit Reviews**. Work you have completed can be stored in a SPHE folder or electronically in an e-folder. Your oral literacy is developed using debates, class presentations and small group and class discussions, while your digital literacy is helped by producing videos, making PowerPoint presentations and taking online quizzes and tests. The use of charts, graphs, surveys, percentages and ratios helps to improve your numeracy skills.

We hope that you enjoy and benefit from your time in post-primary school and that *Health and Wellbeing: SPHE 1* helps you to achieve this!

Anne & Nodlaig

Digital Resources

The *Health and Wellbeing: SPHE 1* digital resources will enhance classroom learning by encouraging student participation and engagement. To aid lesson planning, PowerPoints and animations are **referenced in the textbook** using the following icons:

- **PowerPoints** – cover a range of key topics, including settling in at school, dealing with peer pressure and different forms of wellbeing
- **Animations** – pose scenarios for students to discuss in class.

Visit **www.edcolearning.ie** to access the *Health and Wellbeing: SPHE 1* e-book and digital resources, which also include **worksheets** to accompany the animations and **weblinks** for each unit. Plus, **exclusive additional resources and information** are available at **ie.reachout.com/edco**, in partnership with **Reachout.com**.

UNIT **1** How I See Myself and Others

Learning Outcomes:

This unit helps you to:

1 Get to know the students in your class ⚪

2 Get to know your new school ⚪

3 Understand what SPHE (Social, Personal and Health Education) in post-primary school is about ⚪

4 Draw up a set of rules (class contract) for your work in SPHE. ⚪

(Tick these off as you complete them.)

KEY WORDS

Friendship
Routine
Rules
Class contract
Confidentiality

Activity 1

Walk and Talk!
Getting to know your class

Welcome to your new school and your new class. Let's get to know your classmates.

You have five minutes to 'Walk and Talk!' with everyone in your class and to find someone who fits a description in one of the boxes on page 2. Ask them to sign their name in that box. A classmate may only sign your page once. Don't worry if you don't remember all the names. You will get to know everyone in your class as time goes on. When you have finished or when the five minutes are up, complete the Learning Log.

Find someone who . . .

Was born outside Ireland	Plays a musical instrument	Likes to paint . . .	Is a vegetarian
Has the same birth sign as you	Lives on your road	Lives in a family of five or more people	Did Irish dancing
Is an only child	Has a twin	Loves to bake	Hopes to go to the Gaeltacht next summer
Has a birthday this month	Likes playing video games	Is a strong swimmer	Can speak another language
Has the same number of brothers and sisters as you	Is in a choir	Went abroad this summer	Has a first name with more than eight letters
Doesn't drink tea or coffee	Won an award in primary school	Plays on a team	Read more than three books this summer
Has an unusual pet	Cycles to school	Likes Chinese food	Has brown eyes

Friendship Tips

Sometimes it is not easy to get to know new people so here are some tips and ideas that might help you get started. You will learn more about friendship in future SPHE classes.

Tips for teens on making friends

- Don't try too hard, be yourself, relax
- Be friendly, smile and make eye contact with others
- Show you are interested and take the first step
- Make a special effort to remember your classmates' names
- Ask questions and share a little about yourself too
- Be a good listener

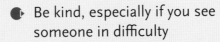
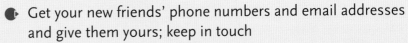

- Be kind, especially if you see someone in difficulty
- Get your new friends' phone numbers and email addresses and give them yours; keep in touch
- Have fun with your new friends but don't forget old friends
- Don't leave people out because they seem different from you
- Don't be cruel, gossip or spread rumours
- Accept people as they are.

LEARNING LOG

I enjoyed the Walk and Talk activity because _____

_____

_____

I found this activity difficult because _____

_____

_____

Something interesting I learned about myself is _____

_____

_____

An interesting thing I learned about others is _____

_____

_____

Activity 2

Who's who and what do they do?

After a few weeks you will become familiar with your timetable and the layout of your new school. This activity will help you to learn the names of key adults in your school, what they do in the school, where their room or office is and how they can help you. Write their names in the spaces below.

Year Head

Name: _____

Role: _____

Deputy Principal

Name: _____

Role: _____

Principal

Name: Mary Byrne

Role: Runs the school

Class Tutor

Name: _____

Role: _____

Guidance Counsellor

Name: _____

Role: _____

Chaplain

Name: _____

Role: _____

Home-school Teacher

Name: _____

Role: _____

School Secretary

Name: _____

Role: _____

School Shop

Name: _____

Role: _____

Caretaker

Name: _____

Role: _____

Canteen Person

Name: _____

Role: _____

Breakfast Club Organiser

Name: _____

Role: _____

Now that you know the names of some key people in your school find out a little more about them. In groups of four, between this class and the next time you have SPHE, interview one of these key people (your teacher will tell you which one). If your school has a school camera find out if you can use it to photograph the person you are interviewing, with their permission of course.

If it is not possible to interview them you could design a short questionnaire and ask them to complete it for you.

Name:

Title:

What do you do?:

Room number:

How I make an appointment:

Available times:

Design a poster or make a short presentation to your class about the person you have interviewed.

If you make a presentation you can keep it in your e-folder. Keep your poster in your SPHE folder.

LEARNING LOG

Activity 3

Taking charge
My guide to sorting things out

Finding your feet in a new school can sometimes be very hard and you will have many questions during the first few weeks. This activity will help you to get answers to some of these questions.

In groups of four, see if you can decide what to do if you found yourself in the situations below. Write your answers in your copybook.

PowerPoint

1. If I forget to bring the right books for English class I . . .
2. If I cannot find my way to the Science Lab I . . .
3. If I lose my locker key I . . .
4. If I forget my PE gear I . . .
5. If I am late for school I . . .
6. If I find a subject too hard I . . .
7. If I am absent from school I . . .
8. If I forget my lunch or lunch money I . . .
9. If I have to carry around a large amount of money for several classes I . . .
10. If I want to get involved in sports or games after school I . . .
11. If I get sick in school I . . .
12. If I need to speak with the school counsellor I . . .
13. If I need to go to the toilet during class I . . .
14. If I forget to do my homework I . . .
15. If I am bullied by someone I . . .
16. If I see someone bullying someone else I . . .
17. If I lose my timetable I . . .
18. If I forget to bring my school journal to class I . . .
19. If I spill something on my uniform and it isn't ready for school I . . .
20. If I need to leave school early I . . .

Don't worry if you can't answer all the questions now. Your subject teachers will help you answer them as you go along. You can also ask your class teacher or year head if you need to. If other people in your school have answers that are helpful, then write them in your copybook as well.

KEY WORDS

Routine
A regular way of doing things in a particular order.

Activity 4

Looking forward

By now you will be more familiar with your school and your new routine. You will have many hopes and maybe also some worries about the future. The pictures below show suns and clouds. The suns represent things that you can look forward to and your hopes for your time in your new school. Write your hopes into the suns. The clouds represent some worries or fears that you might still be a little anxious about. Write these worries into the clouds.

Share what you have written with another student and then read about their hopes and worries.

With another pair, see if you can come up with some ideas that might help you to achieve your hopes and help with your worries. Think about who and what might help.

A Classroom Mood Board

Make a classroom 'mood board'. On one side of a display board, place a large cloud; on the other side insert a big sun. As a class, write the words you came up with in the last activity and fill in the class 'sun and cloud' mood board.

You could write these feelings down on post-its and stick them onto the pictures of the sun and cloud. Then see if you can come up with tips or strategies to help people who are under a cloud to feel better, for example by joining a group, finding something to do, exercising in the fresh air, talking to a friend.

A hope I have, starting in my new school is

To make sure this happens I will

A concern I had starting in my new school was

To help me with this I will

To help someone who is 'under a cloud feel better' I will

Activity 5

Building on the work of primary SPHE

Let's see what you can remember from SPHE in your primary school

In groups of four make a collage illustrating what you remember about SPHE in primary school. You can use pictures from magazines, words, drawings or symbols to do this. In the collage write down what you enjoyed about SPHE in primary school and why.

When your collage is finished, scan it and keep it in your e-folder or keep the original in your SPHE folder.

SPHE in primary school!

SPHE in primary school!

SPHE in your New School

Through SPHE you will learn about yourself and others and how to look after your own health and wellbeing as you move from primary to post-primary school and from childhood to adulthood. Everything you learn in SPHE will link together like a jigsaw and you will explore all these topics over the next three years as you complete the junior cycle.

Strand 1, Who am I?
- You develop your sense of self-awareness and build your self-esteem and that of others
- Your development and the changes you will experience throughout adolescence
- You learn how to manage and organise your life
- You appreciate your rights and the rights of others to live in a safe and inclusive environment.

Strand 2, Minding Myself and Others
- You discover how you can take care of yourself and of others
  - Your physical health
  - Your awareness of smoking, alcohol and addiction
  - You learn how you can develop respectful communication
  - Your understanding of bullying.

Strand 3, Team Up
- You look at the important relationships in your life and learn some skills for building and nurturing these relationships
- You learn about your sexual development
- Your life and media influences

Strand 4, My Mental Health
- You explore ways in which you can build your positive mental health
- You look at young people's experience of mental ill-health and learn how to support yourself and others in tough times.

KEY WORDS

Rule
A rule tells us what is or is not allowed in a particular situation. Rules guide us in what we say or do.

Rules

In almost all areas of our lives we have rules and regulations to help us manage our lives in a safe and fair way. For example, you queue up when waiting for a bus so that the people who were there first get on the bus first. When people don't queue and break this rule there is chaos, as everyone tries to push their way onto the bus at the same time.

Activity 6

Why have rules?

To ensure that we stay safe while using the roads we follow the 'Rules of the Road'. Complete the table below on why we have these rules. The first one is done for you.

Clue	Rule	Reason for rule
Using a zebra crossing	Cross a busy road here	It's safe to cross as drivers will know that you might be crossing
Walking on a country road where there is no footpath		
Wearing seat belts		

Activity 7

School rules

Now let's look at some of the rules we have in school and why we have them. Complete the grid below.

Clue	Rule	Reason for rule
Homework	You must have required homework completed for class each day	It helps you remember what you learned in class and both you and your teacher can see how you are progressing
Absence note		
Recycling bins on corridors		
School uniform		Gives us a sense of identity and belonging

Did You Know?

Sometimes there are specific rules for a particular subject. In SPHE you might be working on your own or with another student or as part of a group, depending on the topic. Each person will have something to contribute and having a clear set of rules will guide how you work.

KEY WORDS

Class contract

An agreement about how we will behave in a respectful way towards each other in our SPHE class.

Activity

8

SPHE class ground rules
Some rules for working together in SPHE

This activity helps you draw up some ground rules which will make it easier for you to work together happily and safely in your SPHE classes throughout the year.

In the table below you are given two important rules to get you started. Working with two of your classmates see if you can agree on three other rules that you would like to see included on a list of ground rules. Your class will then agree on a set of rules for everyone.

Rule	Reason
Listen while someone is speaking	It is important to hear what others are saying
Confidentiality	What someone says in class should not be talked about outside the class. People must be able to speak without fear of what they say being passed on to others

PowerPoint

When your class has agreed on a set of rules, write them on the charter on the opposite page. Then design a class poster, to be signed by everyone, illustrating the rules. Your class poster can be displayed in the SPHE classroom at the start of each class so you don't forget the rules.

Ground Rules –
Our Class Contract

I _____ agree to keep the following

rules so that our SPHE class will be a happy and

safe place for all.

_____

_____

_____

_____

_____

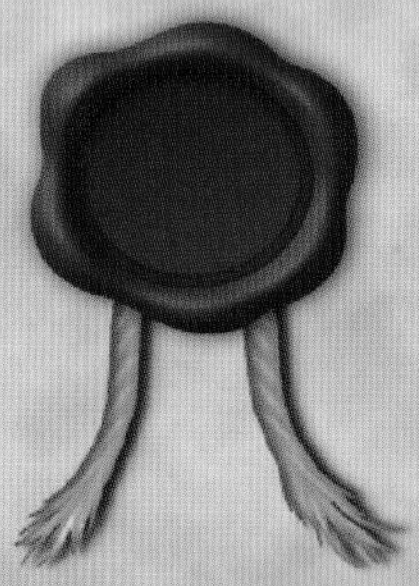

_____
Signed

_____
Date

KEY WORDS

Confidentiality

Confidentiality is a very important part of SPHE. Some things are personal and it might not be suitable to talk about them in a general class discussion. If you are worried or unsure about something it is best to talk, in private, with a parent, a trusted adult or a teacher. Remember that your teacher cannot promise to keep what you say confidential. If they feel that you are at risk they have to tell the principal.

LEARNING LOG

The rule I think I will find easiest to keep is

because

A rule that I might find really tough to keep is

because

I promise to do my best to keep to our agreed rules because

Activity 9

Appreciating difference
Our class tree

As you get to know everyone in your class you will find that some of your classmates have lots in common with you and others will be different from you.

Think about what you bring to the class and any gifts and talents that you might have. Maybe you are good at a particular sport or play a musical instrument. You may be a good listener to your friends or maybe you are always upbeat and in a good mood. Possibly you are someone who has a gift for bringing people together so that everyone feels included. In this activity you'll learn about and appreciate others a little better.

The pictures of the leaf, flower, fruit, water and bug are symbols of things about you. Write on the symbols as follows:

● On the leaf write your first name.

● On the flower write your hopes for your time in school.

● On the fruit write a talent you bring to your class.

On the water write something that would help your class to become a good place to be.

In the speech bubble beside the bug write something that might make your class an unhappy place to be.

Completing your class tree is a reminder of how different each person is and how everyone should value their own and everyone else's talents and gifts.

- Using coloured paper (or a hand-out from your teacher) draw and cut out a large fruit and copy on to it what you have written on the fruit in your book.

- Draw a large class tree and stick your fruit on to it, along with the fruit of the other students in your class.

- Do the same for the leaf, water drop, flower and bug. On the tree you'll have the names, talents and hopes of all those in the class. It also shows the things (bugs) that make your class less enjoyable.

- Bin the bugs to show that everyone will try to stop any 'bugs' from upsetting the work of the class.

A name from my class that I would like to learn more about is
because

A talent or gift that I am glad is in our group is

A talent from those on the tree that I'd like to have myself is

My biggest contribution to this group will be

LEARNING LOG

Assessment – Check your learning

Write a letter to a sixth class student in primary school giving them some advice about settling in to first year in post-primary school. Keep your letter in your SPHE folder or type your letter and save to your e-folder.

Useful Websites

www.childline.ie – a 24-hour listening service for young people up to 18 years of age, open 365 days a year

www.wikihow.com – do a search for 'fit in at a new school' and you will get useful hints and tips on settling into your new school

Review of Unit 1: *How I See Myself and Others*

1. In this unit I learned about _____

_____

_____

2. I think that this will help me when _____

_____

_____

3. In this unit I liked _____

_____

_____

4. In this unit I did not like _____

_____

_____

5. I would like to find out more about _____

_____

_____

6. This unit links with (name another unit in SPHE or another subject) _____

_____

_____

UNIT **2** Self-Management

Learning Outcomes:

This unit helps you to:

1 Learn how to manage your time ○

2 Discover new ways to study effectively ○

3 Appreciate the importance of having balance in your life ○

4 Understand the importance of keeping yourself safe at home, on the road, out and about and online. ○

(Tick these off as you complete them.)

Did You Know?

We forget 44 per cent of what we learn in the first 20 minutes! Within 24 hours, if we have not studied the information that we learned in class, we will have forgotten 80 per cent of it!

KEY WORDS

Homework
Study
Time management
Timetable
A balanced life
Personal safety
Fire safety
Road safety
ICE (In Case of Emergency)
Cyber safety

Activity

1 Managing my time in school

KEY WORDS

Homework

Work given by your teacher to be completed by a specific date.

Study

To revise information and material to ensure you know what you need to know well.

Research shows that how well you study is strongly linked to your success in exams. Do the quiz below to find out how well you are managing the time you spend on your homework. Read these statements and think about whether you agree, disagree or are unsure about them. Then tick whichever box fits your answer.

Homework quiz

	Agree	Disagree	Unsure
You should start your homework as soon as you get home from school.			
It is important that the room you study in is warm.			
Listening to music affects how you study.			
It is okay to have your mobile phone with you while you study.			
You should take a break every 30 minutes.			
You should always do learning homework before written homework.			
It is not a good idea to have a 'study free' day at the weekend.			
You should spend the same amount of time on each subject.			
Homework should always be done on the night it is given.			
You should start your homework with the subject you like least.			
If you run into a problem with a particular subject you should stick at it until you get it sorted out.			
Your study session should always include some revision.			

 **PowerPoint**

After you have taken the homework quiz, with your teacher and classmates explore ways for you all to study more efficiently. Write down three changes that you need to make so you will get more out of the time you spend doing your homework and studying.

1 _____

_____

2 _____

_____

3 _____

_____

KEY WORDS

Time management

Using your time is about using your time effectively so that the right amount of time is allocated to each activity that you need to do.

My name is Sally and I'm a first-year student in Ballydavid Community School. I love my new school and am getting on well there. But I do have a few worries about how to manage my homework and study as it is all quite different from primary school. I love French, especially the conversation pieces. English is my least favourite subject as there are so many different areas to study and it takes ages to finish my homework.

I have a busy life outside school too and have to make time for catching up with my friends, dance classes (Monday 6.15–7.00pm), football training (I'm on the local team) and of course my favourite TV programmes. I love Saturdays as I can often lie in, and sometimes I earn some money by minding my sister's children on Saturday afternoons. I also have to tidy my room and help with the chores at home. I often meet my friends in one of their houses on a Saturday evening for a chat or we sometimes go to the cinema.

Activity 2

Sally's Monday timetable

Below is the timetable for a typical Monday in Sally's life. Look at her school timetable and the study timetable she has drawn up for Monday after school. Then answer the questions.

My Mad Monday

8.50am	Registration
9.00am	Irish
9.40am	English
10.20am	Digital Media
10.55am	Break
11.05am	Maths
11.40am	Science
12.15pm	Science
1.00pm	Lunch
1.40pm	PE
2.20pm	PE
3.00pm	French
3.40pm	Home

Here is my homework and study timetable for Monday evening. I wrote down my homework throughout the day so I'm clear about what I have to do.

4.00–4.30pm	Chats with friends and taking a short break and a snack before settling down to study
4.30–5.00pm	English (As this is my least favourite subject I get it out of the way!)
5.00–5.30pm	Irish
5.30–6.00pm	Maths
6.15–7.00pm	Dance class (a five-minute walk from my home)
7.15–7.45pm	Dinner
7.45–8.00pm	Digital Media (I have to rehearse my part in a small presentation my group is making on Wednesday. I love this subject and I've done a lot of work on it already.)
8.00–8.30pm	French (I am quite tired by now but I love French so I find it easy enough to finish off my homework.)

Note!

Even though Sally has science homework from today's class she doesn't have Science again until Thursday. She has made a note in her journal to complete that homework on Tuesday afternoon as she knows she will have time then. She does not have homework in all the subjects that day.

1 Why do you think Sally planned her timetable like this?

_____

_____

2 What do you like about Sally's homework timetable?

_____

_____

3 What would you do differently, if you were Sally?

_____

_____

Activity 3

My study timetable

Using what you have learned in the previous activities, Homework quiz and Sally's Monday timetable, write an after-school study timetable for yourself for a whole week. Don't forget to add in meal times, and any activities you have outside school including scouts, training, music, 'must see' TV programmes and so on.

KEY WORDS

Timetable
A plan of things you have to do and the times you will do them.

Study Plan

Time	Monday	Tuesday	Wednesday	Thursday	Friday	Saturday
3.30pm						
4.00pm						
4.30pm						
5.00pm						
5.30pm						
6.00pm						
6.30pm						
7.00pm						
7.30pm						
8.00pm						
8.30pm						
9.00pm						

The Three S's of Effective Study

Stuff – **what you need.** Make sure you have everything you need to start studying, including books, copies, flash cards, pens and highlighters.

Schedule – **when you do your work.** Have you planned what you will do? Have you made a note of when the homework needs to be completed? Use your study timetable to work out your schedule.

Space – **where you work.** Think about lighting and room temperature. Is your desk cluttered or organised? Have you a homework timetable or planner on the wall?

Is your study area free of distractions?

Is your phone turned off?

The three S's:
Stuff
Schedule
Space

Think about how you approach your homework and complete this Learning Log.

Two things I do well in my homework and study are:

1

2

Two things that I can do to improve my study habits are:

1

2

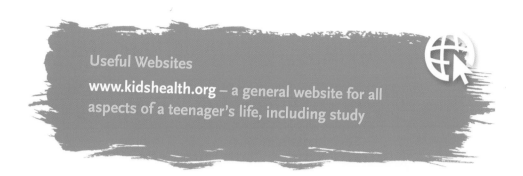

Useful Websites

www.kidshealth.org – a general website for all aspects of a teenager's life, including study

Balance in My Life

You have learned how to plan and organise your homework so that you are ready for class and your school life is organised, but what about the rest of your life? Do you make time for your friends? Do you get enough rest? Could your life be healthier if you had more balance in it?

KEY WORDS

A Balanced Life?

A balanced life means that you make time for all the different elements that make up a healthy life. This includes **work** (school, homework and study, helping with jobs at home), **rest** (sleep and relaxation) and **play** (sports, music, reading, meeting friends and so on).

A healthy lifestyle is one where you feel fit and well, mentally, physically, socially and spiritually.

BALANCE YOUR LIFE

Social health involves spending time with your family and friends, joining a club, having hobbies and doing fun activities like playing in a football team or being in a band.

Physical health includes making sure you exercise, have a good diet and nutrition, and rest and relaxation.

Emotional (mental) health includes dealing with your feelings, managing stress, having fun, knowing when to ask for help and making sure you ask for it.

Spiritual health refers to the things that give meaning and purpose to your life. It might be your beliefs and values, your religion, praying, meditation, mindfulness, yoga and so on.

The results of leading a healthy and balanced lifestyle mean that:

1   You get enough exercise, eat healthily and avoid getting involved in drugs.

2   You are able to talk to others about your worries and problems and not bottle them up until they cause stress and anxiety.

3   You make time for meeting your friends, having fun and enjoying your hobbies, as well as building in time for schoolwork and work at home.

4   You make sure you get enough sleep, rest, relaxation and find other ways to recharge your batteries.

tips

If you lead a balanced life you are more likely to be happier, healthier, less stressed and more fulfilled.

4

Health check
What does it mean to be healthy?

1 Come up with as many words as you can that describe what being healthy means to you and write them below.

_____
_____
_____
_____
_____
_____
_____
_____

2 Now write the words under the headings Physical, Mental/Emotional, Social and Spiritual Health.

Physical health	Emotional/Mental health	Social health	Spiritual health

REMEMBER

Remember a balanced and healthy life has factors of all four elements of health in it!

25

Activity 5

A healthy lifestyle is a balanced lifestyle

Get into groups of four and have a look at the pictures of Tim, Tom, Trish and Tanya below. In your group decide who you think has the most balanced lifestyle and why.

TIM

Tim loves school and has no problem with the work. He likes to be top of his class and is an 'A' student in most subjects. At the start of first year he decided to give up sports to concentrate on his studies. He continues to play his guitar, mostly on his own.

TANYA

Tanya is a popular girl who is just as happy being on her own or with her friends. She manages to keep up with her work in school because she's organised. Tanya is on the local football team and needs to train two evenings a week. Her friends say she is a good listener and they can rely on her. After a busy day Tanya likes to wind down by spending some time in a quiet place, listening to relaxing music.

TOM

Tom is 17 years old and wants to be an international soccer player so he never misses an opportunity to train. This means he is hardly ever at home with his family and, apart from the team, he is losing contact with his friends Fulfilling his ambition has taken over Tom's life.

TRISH

Trish joined first year a little late in the year so she found it hard to get to know the other pupils in her class. She is quite shy and doesn't try to join in with the rest of her class. Trish goes home at lunchtime and watches TV alone while having her lunch. She has lots of friends on Facebook.

1. We think the person who has the most balanced lifestyle is _____ because

_____

2. We think the person who has the least balanced lifestyle is _____ because

_____

6 A day in Pat's life

1 Read Pat's story below and working with two of your classmates decide what advice you would give to Pat to make his life more balanced.

2 Find the words in the story that show how Pat is leading a healthy life and how his life is not so healthy. Mark these in two different colours and use what you have marked to finish sentences (a) and (b) below.

(a) Pat's lifestyle is healthy because _____

_____

_____

(b) Pat could make his lifestyle healthier by _____

_____

_____

Pat's Tuesday

It is 4pm on Tuesday and school is over. Pat can't wait to get home to meet up with his friends. They might play football or listen to some music. Pat knows that there is homework to be done and the essay he got last Friday is still unfinished. Pat quickly changes out of his uniform and heads for the green to meet his friends. He tells himself he will stay out for an hour, come home, have dinner and then tackle his homework.

However, one of Pat's friends, Mark, has just got a new PlayStation and he suggests that they all go to his house to play some games. Pat loses track of time and before he knows it two hours have passed and he is late home for dinner. Never mind, he thinks, there is still lots of time to get the homework for tomorrow done and that dreaded essay finished.

On the way home, Pat remembers that his mother is at the gym and has left him some salad and soup in the fridge. He doesn't like this food at all, so he goes to the takeaway for a burger and chips.

After dinner Pat starts his homework. He checks his journal to see what needs to be done. Although he had a maths class today there is no homework recorded. Strange, as maths homework is given every night. He decides to ring Sarah and get his maths homework from her. Pat does his French homework first, as he doesn't like French and wants to get it over with.

Pat's Tuesday continued

Next comes science. Pat loves science as there is a lot of practical work. Today's homework is to write up the experiment done in class today. He spends a long time doing the drawings and takes pride in the results.

It is now 8.45pm and Pat's favourite TV programme is on at 9pm. He considers finishing the English essay while he watches TV. But, he is tired now and decides to catch up on both the English essay and the maths in the morning. He will go into school early and do the maths before classes start. Luckily for Pat, English is at 2pm, so Pat decides to finish his essay during lunch break.

At 10.15pm Pat goes to bed, but first he organises his books for the next day, checking his subjects against his timetable. Pat realises he has PE at 9.40am and has to find his gear. He decides to leave this until the morning. As a result, Pat is late leaving home so he has no chance of getting his maths homework done in time for class and he is worried. He decides not to let this situation happen again.

No sooner has Pat arrived in school than the bell for roll-call rings and a new day has started.

Our advice to Pat is _____

_____

_____

_____

_____

_____

_____

_____

_____

_____

_____

Being well
What floats your boat?

Earlier in this unit you learned that looking after your general wellbeing means caring for different elements of your health. This includes your physical health, your emotional and mental health, your social health and your spiritual health. A healthy lifestyle has a nice balance between all areas.

The raft on the right represents your wellbeing. It needs to be balanced if it is to stay afloat. On each of the barrels write in two things that you can do to make your life more balanced in that particular area. Then complete the Learning Log.

LEARNING LOG

One change I will make so that my life becomes more balanced is

To do this I need to

Something or somebody who could help me here is

Having a balanced life is important to me because

Becoming Independent
Keeping yourself safe at home, on the road and online

Personal safety

Learning to become independent is an important part of growing up. Keeping yourself safe while you start doing things by yourself is essential to maintaining your health and wellbeing. You may think that nothing can harm you, but you need to be aware of the problems that may arise if you do put your personal safety at risk. This applies to your safety when you are at **home**, on the **road** and also when you are out and about in **cyberspace**.

Fire safety

Each year an average of 40 people die in fires in Ireland, mostly in house fires. The Fire Brigade answers almost 50,000 calls every year. With a little more thought and awareness of basic safety procedures at home, many of these fires could have been prevented and lives could have been spared.

REMEMBER

Safety in school

Your school will have a fire safety procedure and you will probably have practised a fire drill. If you hear the fire alarm, leaving your classroom in a safe and orderly way ensures that nobody will be injured and everyone gets out safely.

During the next week think about the classrooms you are in for different subjects and be sure that you know the evacuation procedure for each room. If you are unsure then ask your teacher.

Activity 8

Fire safety at home

Have a look at the picture below and identify the fire risks that you see. There are at least ten. Highlight them in red.

Fire Safety Dos and Don'ts

Do

- Talk to an adult about having a smoke alarm (If you have one make sure it is working!)
- Keep all matches and lighters out of the reach of young children
- Use a spark guard in front of your open fire
- Use proper candle holders if you are burning candles and never leave lighted candles unattended
- Put out all candles before you go to bed
- Have a fire extinguisher and a fire blanket in your kitchen
- Close all internal doors at night
- Make sure you know where the safety exits are if you live in a flat or apartment block
- Ask your family to have a practice fire drill so everyone knows how to get out quickly and safely if there is a fire.

PowerPoint

Fire Saftey: Don't

✗ Leave burning candles unattended

✗ Leave your chip pans and frying pans unattended

✗ Dry your clothes by hanging them close to an open fire

✗ Use faulty electrical appliances in your house

✗ Overload your electrical sockets.

With an adult, do a 'fire safety check' of your home. Identify three improvements you need to make to ensure your home is a safer place for all your family and write them below. Write these below:

To make my home a safer place we need to:

1

2

3

LEARNING LOG

Road safety

We often take our safety on the road for granted but Irish roads can be dangerous. In 2016, 175 people were killed in accidents on roads around Ireland. Many more are injured every year and some of these victims are disabled for life.

If we all take more care and are safer on our roads, lives would be saved. This applies to pedestrians and cyclists, as much as to drivers.

BE SAFE
WEAR A HELMET

Activity 9

Road hazards

Examine the drawing below and see if you can find seven hazards. Mark each one with a red triangle.

Two new things I learned about fire safety are _____

_____

_____

_____

Two new things I learned about road safety are _____

_____

_____

_____

_____

Activity 10

Journey planner

On a separate A4 page draw a map or use a printed Google map of the route you take to school, either walking or cycling. If you get a lift to school, then work with a classmate who walks/cycles to school.

Mark in the places on your route where you need to take extra care. In the space below write why you need to take extra care in these areas and how you could be safer at this point. Do this for three of the most dangerous parts of your journey.

Here is an example:

Crossing the main road at _____ I need to be watching out for oncoming traffic and for cars pulling out.
I can be safer here by being alert and I have to make sure I'm not distracted by my mobile, listening to music or chatting with friends.

1 _____

_____

2 _____

_____

3 _____

_____

Your safety: staying safe while you're out

We have looked at safety in your home and on the roads. Your safety can also be at risk in other areas. Let's explore some of these areas and you can find out how to keep yourself safe.

Activity 11

The danger zone

Each day we can find ourselves in risky situations without being aware of them. Think about what it is that makes a situation dangerous and have a look at the examples listed below. Then in the last row write in two examples of situations you feel are dangerous.

With a partner rank the dangerous situations in order of 1 to 12, with 1 being the most dangerous and 12 being the least dangerous. Then join with another pair and try to come to an agreement about which four you all think are the most dangerous situations

Dangerous situations			
Situation	Ranking	Situation	Ranking
Being robbed or mugged		Cycling without a helmet	
Being threatened while alone		Fighting on the road	
Being bullied by text messages		Regularly eating from takeaways	
Having nasty comments made about you on Facebook		Texting while walking on the road	
Being in an unsafe situation while working on a farm		Getting money from an ATM machine while someone you don't know is looking over your shoulder	
_____		_____	

We agree that the four most risky situations are:

1. _____ because _____
2. _____ because _____
3. _____ because _____
4. _____ because _____

Tips for staying safe while you are out and about

- If possible, avoid situations where you have to walk home alone at night
- Always tell someone where you are going, who you will be with and what time you will be home
- Make sure you have your mobile phone, with credit on it, with you when going out
- Always wait for your bus or train in a place that is well lit
- Sit near other passengers on bus, DART, Luas or train journeys so they will hear you if you call for help
- Have extra money with you in case you get stranded somewhere (hide a €5 note in your inside pocket – just in case)
- Look confident and be alert to what is going on around you
- Avoid poorly lit alleys and roads
- If you have to take a taxi, text the number of the taxi to a parent or trusted adult
- Wear a 'high-vis' jacket or reflector belt if you are walking outside at night
- If you think you are being followed ring 999 or contact a trusted adult. Have their number under ICE (In Case of Emergency) on your phone.

LEARNING LOG

Find out how to set up an ICE – In Case of Emergency number on your phone.
This can be used even when your phone is locked.
Memorise the number of a parent or guardian to be contacted if you don't have your own phone or if you have lost it.

Cyber safety while online and using your mobile phone

Most of you have mobile phones and many of you have smartphones where you can be online all the time, depending on your credit. While the internet can sometimes be a very useful source of information, being online does have some risks. You know that you should never open the door to strangers at home, and the same goes for the internet. Only chat to people online whose names you recognise.

It is important not to take any chances while online and that you know how to stay safe. You also need to know what you should do if you feel upset or unsafe.

KEY WORDS

Cyber safety
Learning how to keep safe while you are online.

12 Staying safe in cyberspace

Read the tips below for staying safe while online or using your mobile phone. Then work with a partner to come up with a reason for each of these and write your answer in the space below.

- Treat others on the internet as you would like to be treated because _____

_____

- Avoid signing-in to chatrooms unless they are monitored for bullying and other unsuitable behaviour because _____

_____

_____

- Tell a trusted adult if you come across something unpleasant, which makes you feel uncomfortable or upsets you because _____

_____

_____

- Only give your mobile number to family and friends because _____

_____

_____

- If you receive hurtful text messages tell a trusted adult because _____

_____

_____

- Never give out personal information such as your name, address, mobile number, birth date, school's name or parents/guardians' names because _____

_____

- Never send an online picture of yourself, even if someone sends you one of themselves because

  _____

  _____

- Never trust someone who says they know you or your friends if you don't recognise them because _____

  _____

  _____

- Never arrange to meet up with someone you meet online and who you don't know because _____

  _____

  _____

  _____

  _____

REMEMBER

If you are worried about anything that happens to you while you are on your mobile phone or online, ask for help from your parent or guardian.

LEARNING LOG

With two classmates, create a poster, to be put up in your school, on the theme 'Let's keep safe on the internet'.

_____

_____

Think about what you and your friends can do to stay safe on the internet. Be as creative as you can.

_____

_____

Assessment – Check your learning

In groups of four make a short presentation for first-year students outlining either option 1 or 2 below:

1 How to make good use of homework and study time.

2 How to make sure that they lead a balanced lifestyle that helps them cope with the new demands of post-primary school.

You could present this in a variety of ways including a PowerPoint presentation, a one-page leaflet or an oral presentation to your class.

Useful Websites

www.kidshealth.org – the 'teenhealth' section of this website offers helpful advice to teenagers on all aspects of growing up, including staying safe

www.suzylamplugh.org – aims to raise awareness of the importance of personal safety and gives help and advice on the best ways to be safe

Review of Unit 2: *Self-Management*

1 In this unit I learned about _____
_____
_____

2 I think that this will help me when _____
_____
_____

3 In this unit I liked _____
_____
_____

4 In this unit I did not like _____
_____
_____

5 I would like to find out more about _____
_____
_____

6 This unit links with (name another unit in SPHE or another subject) _____
_____
_____

UNIT 3 — Being an Adolescent

Learning Outcomes:

This unit helps you to:

① Understand that adolescence is a time of gradual change between childhood and adulthood ◯

② Learn about the emotional, social, psychological and physical changes that take place during adolescence ◯

③ Recognise the physical changes that take place in boys and girls during puberty ◯

④ Understand the parts of the male and female reproductive systems and how they work. ◯

(Tick each topic off as you complete it.)

KEY WORDS

Adolescence
Puberty
Physical changes
Emotional Changes
Psychological changes
Social changes
Reproduction

Changes during adolescence

Your first year in post-primary school is a time of great change:

● Your body is changing – **physical changes**

● Your mind is changing – **psychological changes**

● Your feelings are changing – **emotional changes**

● Your relationships with family and friends are changing – **social changes**.

KEY WORDS

Adolescence
The time between puberty and adulthood.

Did You Know?

Girls usually start puberty somewhere between nine and fourteen years of age, but it may begin and end earlier or later.

Boys usually start puberty a little later than girls, sometime between ten and fifteen years of age.

KEY WORDS

Puberty
The time when your body physically changes from a child's body to the body of a young man or woman. These changes happen gradually, over a number of years.

Activity

1 Teenagers: all the same – all different

Look at the group of teenagers in the photograph below. They are all the same age. What do you notice about them?

_____

_____

_____

_____

REMEMBER

Puberty can be a confusing time! Everyone changes at his/her own rate. Some of you will begin to change much earlier or later than others and that is normal. There is no right or wrong time to begin puberty. If you have any worries about this, talk to a parent/guardian or an adult that you trust.

PowerPoint

Changes at Puberty

Let's look at some of the changes that you can expect. You will learn more about these changes in other areas of SPHE (Social, Personal and Health Education).

Psychological (mental) changes

As you get older you are beginning to think more like an adult. You are getting to know yourself and develop your own identity. You wish to be more independent.

You think about things more seriously and you begin to have your own ideas, opinions and values. This can be confusing and sometimes can cause friction if your ideas and opinions are different from those of your parents/guardians, friends or society in general.

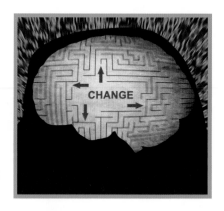

Social changes

During adolescence your friendships and relationships often change. You may make new friends and have one or two close friends who are going through the same experiences as yourself so you have a lot in common. You might become interested in having a boyfriend or girlfriend. You may feel that your relationship with your family is changing as you become more independent.

This might be difficult for you at a time when your parents feel you are not yet ready. One minute you want to be treated as an adult and the next as a child. Explaining to your parents/guardians how you feel can be helpful, especially if they see you are willing to be more responsible. Changes in your relationships with friends and family can be confusing and difficult to understand at times but they are all part of growing up.

Emotional changes

Emotional changes during adolescence are often hardest to deal with. You might experience very strong feelings at different times and sometimes you might find yourself 'flying off the handle' for no real reason. At times you may experience mood swings which you find difficult to understand or control. All of this is as a result of the hormones (chemical messengers) your body is producing to bring about other changes in your body. Dealing with these different emotions may be difficult at the time, but remember, it will soon pass.

Physical changes

Let's look at the physical changes in more detail!

 The HSE 'Busy Bodies' series of animations introduce the physical changes that happen during puberty. You can find them at www.healthpromotion.ie/health/inner/busy_bodies.

Did You Know?

During puberty your body will grow faster than at any other stage in your life, except for your first year.

Here's how it begins!

During adolescence a gland in your brain, the pituitary gland, sends chemical messengers, called hormones through your blood stream. The hormones go to different parts of your body, triggering other changes: in boys the testes begin to make the male hormone testosterone, and in girls the ovaries begin to make the female hormones oestrogen and progesterone.

The pituitary gland also makes a growth hormone which causes bones and muscles to grow faster during puberty.

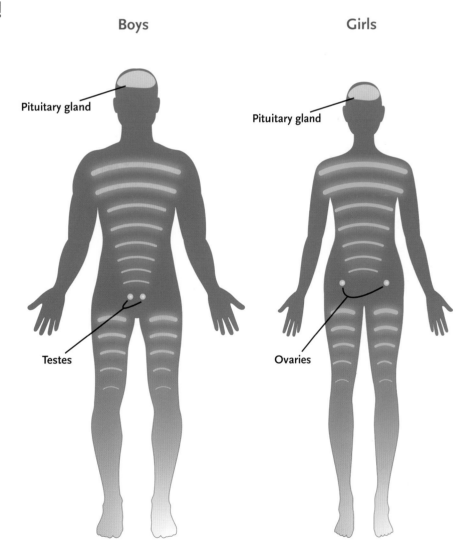

Boys

Pituitary gland

Testes

Girls

Pituitary gland

Ovaries

Physical changes in boys

- Body shape changes. Arms and legs lengthen and muscles develop

- Skin becomes oily. Pores may become blocked, resulting in spots or acne on face, neck and back

- Voice deepens (known as voice 'breaking')

- More perspiration

- Hair growth on face, arms, legs, chest and around the penis (pubic hair)

- Penis grows longer and thicker

- Testes grow larger and begin to produce sperm

- Sometimes boys will start to get erections (when the penis fills with blood and becomes hard)

- Wet dreams may happen when the penis becomes erect while a boy is sleeping and a liquid called semen escapes. This is called ejaculation.

Activity

2 About a boy – the Reproductive System

Now that you know about the changes that occur in boys at puberty, write in everything that you can remember on this outline. Remember to include changes that are not so easily seen – the emotional, social and psychological changes.

While obvious changes are happening on the outside of a boy's body there are also other changes happening on the inside. A boy's reproductive system is maturing too. The diagram below shows what it looks like. Draw a line from each label to the correct part of the diagram.

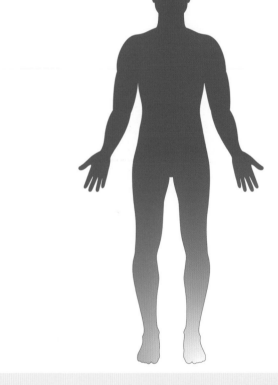

Scrotum: holds the testes

Testes: produce sperm

Penis: contains the urethra, which carries urine and semen outside the body, and is involved in sexual intercourse

Sperm duct: carries sperm from testes through the urethra outside the body

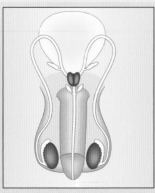

Bladder: holds urine

Seminal vesicles: provide fluid for sperm to swim in

Prostate gland: produces fluid that nourishes the sperm

Urethra: carries urine and sperm outside the body (not both at the same time)

Physical changes in girls

- Body shape changes – hips widen, causing body to become curvier
- Weight may increase
- Breasts gradually develop
- More perspiration
- Skin becomes oily. Pores may become blocked, resulting in spots or acne on face, neck and back.

- Hair growth under arms and between legs (pubic hair)
- Menstruation (periods) begins
- Wall of the vagina thickens and starts to produce mucus.

Activity 3

About a girl – the Reproductive System

Now that you know about the changes that occur in girls during puberty, write the details onto the outline. Remember to include changes that are not so easily seen – the emotional, social and psychological ones. You can use words or symbols to describe the changes.

While obvious changes are happening on the outside of a girl's body there are also other changes happening on the inside. A girl's reproductive system is maturing too. In the diagram below you can see what it looks like. Draw a line from each label to the correct part of the diagram.

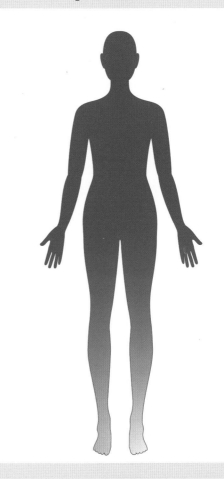

Ovaries: produce eggs

Vagina: muscular tube that connects uterus (womb) to outside of the body

Cervix: neck of the uterus

Fallopian tubes: carry egg from ovary to the uterus

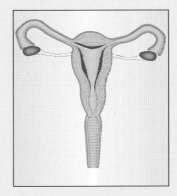

Lining of the womb: a build-up of blood which receives the fertilised egg. If no fertilisation occurs the egg is released from the body during menstruation (period)

Uterus (womb): a baby grows and develops here during pregnancy

Did You Know?

The changes that take place in your body during puberty are preparing you physically so that you can become a father or a mother when you are older. Just because your body is physically ready to become a parent, however, doesn't mean that you are mentally or emotionally ready. During puberty a lot of other, non-physical changes are taking place as well, for example in the way that you relate to other people, especially your family.

This process of change takes several years throughout your adolescence and lasts until you become an adult and are then ready to become a parent. You will learn more about this in Strand 3.

LEARNING LOG

Think about the changes that take place during adolescence and how you feel about them, and complete your log.

One thing that is good about being an adolescent is

One thing I find difficult about being an adolescent is

If I have a concern about some aspect of being an adolescent I can

Assessment – Check your learning

You have been asked to write a short feature for a popular magazine aimed at young teenagers. The title is 'Adolescence – what's it all about?'. Using the websites below, research and write about one of the changes that young people experience at this time. Save your article to your e-folder or in your SPHE folder.

Useful Websites

www.barnardos.ie – Barnardos works to campaign for the rights of children and the teen help part of the site provides hints and tips for teenagers on how they can look after themselves

www.cyh.com – the teen health section of this site gives advice on how you can be a happy and healthy teenager

Review of Unit 3: *Being an Adolescent*

1 In this unit I learned about _____

_____

_____

2 I think that this will help me when _____

_____

_____

3 In this unit I liked _____

_____

_____

4 In this unit I did not like _____

_____

_____

5 I would like to find out more about _____

_____

_____

6 This unit links with (name another unit in SPHE or another subject) _____

_____

_____

UNIT 1 Being Healthy

Being Healthy

In this unit we are going to look at what the phrase 'being healthy' means.

If someone says you have good health it doesn't just mean that you are not sick. It also means that you have a sense of wellbeing (or being well) and feel good about yourself.

Health is a state of complete physical, mental and social wellbeing and not merely the absence of disease or infirmity.

World Health Organization

KEY WORDS

Health – physical, social, mental

Physical activity

Vegetarian

Vegan

Carbohydrates

Proteins

Vitamins

Minerals

Fats

Food pyramid

Eatwell guide

Let's look at the different types of heath that make up your **total health**:

- **Physical health**
- **Mental health**
- **Social health**

Physical health

Physical health (or physical wellbeing) is probably the one you know best. It means feeling well and having the energy to get up every day and do what you have to do, like going to school. It also means getting enough sleep, eating well, feeling fit and being active. Ask yourself: Do I get enough rest? Do I eat the right kinds of foods? Do I feel well? Am I fit?

Mental health

Mental health takes in how much you enjoy life and how good you are at coping with all the things that happen to you. Everyone has disappointments and things which don't work out for them in their lives. Good mental health means you are able to cope with these ups and downs and any stress in your life. Another word for being able to do this is being **resilient**.

Social health

Social health is how you get on with other people. Not everyone will be your friend, but you should be able to communicate and 'get along' with people and be part of a community. If your social health is good, then you are able to make and keep friends, and those friends should make you feel good about yourself. Healthy relationships are based on respect, mutual trust and equality.

Ways to achieve total health

There are many things you can do to improve your physical, mental and social wellbeing:

- You can make good food choices so that you have a healthy and nutritious diet
- You can do things that are important for maintaining your health, such as physical activity, getting enough sleep and rest so that you can cope with the stresses in your life
- You can avoid harmful behaviours such as smoking, drug and alcohol misuse.

Body care

Keeping your body clean is an important part of keeping physically, mentally and socially healthy. If you are dirty you run the risk of picking up diseases and infections. You may also have difficulty making friends and become lonely or isolated.

Activity 1

How much do you know about hygiene?

Do the test below to check how much you know about hygiene. You can use the information on the following two pages to help you.

Draw arrows from the middle column to the correct boxes under 'Why clean' and 'How to clean'.

How to clean		Why clean
Wash with soap every day	NAILS	You sweat a lot here
Change underwear and socks daily	HAIR	You have a large collection of sweat glands here
Use a brush and soapy water	TEETH	Sweat and bacteria turn to bad odours
Wash daily and use deodorant	FEET	Grease and dirt build up
Brush with toothpaste and use floss	UNDERARMS	Sweat and dirt make them smelly
Shampoo and condition Check for lice	SKIN	Tummy bugs and disease are passed on by these
Wash before going to bed	CLOTHES	Trapped food and sugars cause decay and smell bad
Shower regularly, particularly after exercise	HANDS	Dirt is trapped under here

These websites also have good information on hygiene and cleanliness:
www.ndhealthfacts.org
www.kidshealth.org/teen

Keeping clean

Keeping yourself clean is really important. Here is some basic information to help you look and feel your best.

Smelling clean

Body odour increases when you reach puberty. Body smells are caused by:

- Chemicals in sweat
- Waste excreted through the skin
- Bacteria on the skin that feed on dead skin and sweat
- Unwashed clothes, particularly underwear and socks.

Washing

Have a shower or bath every day and use deodorant. Have a wash if you have been sweating and after doing exercise. For girls, it is especially important to shower when you are having your period.

Clothes

Clothes get stained and dirty so you need to wash and change them often. Underwear and socks should be changed every day. They are worn close to the skin and major sweat glands which means that they collect dead skin, sweat and other stains. Bacteria set to work on these stains overnight, and by next morning underwear and socks can smell quite bad.

Feet

The largest collection of sweat glands is on your feet. So wash your feet every day and dry them well.

If you swim a lot be careful about walking around in bare feet as you could pick up fungal infections or verrucas.

Shoes

Shoes wrap tightly around the sweat glands on your feet, which makes them sweat. If you have more than one pair of shoes, alternate them to give them a chance to air.

Hands

Hands attract infections and dirt. Most infections, especially colds and gastroenteritis (tummy bug), are caught by putting unwashed hands into the mouth or handling food with dirty hands. Always wash your hands after using the toilet and before preparing or eating food. Use soap and a nail-brush if your nails are dirty.

Hair

The scalp produces dead skin cells, sweat and oil. When you are washing your hair you should massage the shampoo into your scalp to loosen the dead cells and dirt. Use conditioner if your hair is dry.

Head lice are tiny, wingless insects that live among human hairs and feed on tiny amounts of blood drawn from the scalp. They are a very common problem, especially for young people. They are contagious, annoying, and sometimes tough to get rid of. Get a parent/guardian to check your hair regularly for lice. Treatments that work quickly are available over the counter from your local pharmacy.

Teeth

Food and sugars stay in the mouth and cause tooth decay and bad breath. Brush and floss your teeth at least twice a day, before/after breakfast and before bed.

REMEMBER

If you are clean, you will be healthier and you will also feel more confident and are more likely to have and keep friends.

Did You Know?

In Ancient Rome, famous gladiators scraped accumulated sweat, dirt and grease off their bodies and sold it to their fans in small vials. Roman women reportedly used it as a face cream.

Activity 2

Know your hygiene

Now that you know more about keeping yourself clean, answer the questions below.

1 Did anything you found out about keeping clean surprise you? If yes, what was it?

_____

_____

2 Is there anything in the text about keeping clean that you do not agree with or that you think is incorrect? Why is this?

_____

_____

3 Why do you think some people might have difficulty keeping themselves clean?

_____

_____

4 What advice would you give them?

_____

_____

Activity 3

What would you do?

Did You Know?

The human body is home to over 1,000 species of bacteria. There are more germs on your body than there are people in the United States.

Someone you know has a body odour problem. Here are three ways of dealing with this problem. In each case write what you think the student is feeling and describe how you would feel in that situation. Decide which is the best option.

Option 1

Isolate the person. Nobody sits beside the person or hangs out with him or her.

The student feels _____

_____

_____

I would feel _____

_____

Option 2

Open all the windows and spray air freshener around when the student comes into the room.

The student feels _____

_____

_____

I would feel _____

_____

_____

After being honest with someone about something sensitive it is important that you talk to him/her soon afterwards. This doesn't have to be a long conversation, just a way of letting that person know that you are still friends and that you have moved on from what you talked about.

Option 3

Talk to the student privately and gently suggest that he or she might have a problem with body odour.

The student feels _____

_____

_____

I would feel _____

_____

_____

Write out what you might say in Option 3.

_____

_____

_____

_____

_____

You should now be able to complete the sentences below:

To me, being clean is important because

Something I find hardest about it is

Healthy Eating

It is essential to eat healthily throughout your life but it is especially important in adolescence as you are growing and changing so fast.

Eating well will help you to:

- Stay healthy
- Have more energy
- Achieve mental and social wellbeing.

Your mood and mental functioning are affected by what you eat and being overweight can have a huge effect on a young person's life.

As you get older, your eating patterns usually change. In post-primary school your school day is longer and what you eat for lunch forms a major part of your daily food intake. It is also likely that you will be eating away from home more often because you are spending more time with your friends. Your parents will often allow you to have more say in what you eat so it is vital that you understand exactly what is in food and how it works, so that you can make healthy choices.

Vegetarian

People who do not eat meat or fish are vegetarians. They get protein and some vitamins and minerals from other sources such as cheese, milk, nuts, beans and lentils.

Did You Know?

A student in Florida, USA recently won her school science fair by proving that there are more bacteria in ice machines at fast-food restaurants than in toilet bowl water.

Vegan

A vegan does not eat anything of animal origin. This includes meat and fish and also honey, eggs and all dairy produce.

You Are What You Eat!

What's in food?

Carbohydrates

Most foods contain carbohydrates and they are the major source of energy (fuel) for the body, as it breaks them down into simple sugars. The main foods in this group are grains, wheat, pasta, potatoes and rice.

PowerPoint

Carbohydrates also contain fibre which helps digestion and makes you feel full.

Proteins

Many foods contain protein but the best sources are beef, poultry, fish, eggs, dairy products, nuts, seeds and pulses such as black beans and lentils.

Protein builds, maintains, and replaces the tissues in your body. Many foods high in protein also contain the minerals which the body needs to stay healthy. For example, red meat contains iron which the body uses to make blood.

Vitamins

Vitamins are found in most foods that we eat. They help your body to break down and use the proteins, carbohydrates and fats in food. Your body needs them to work properly, so you grow and develop. When it comes to vitamins, each one has a special role to play. For example:

- Vitamin D in milk is essential for healthy teeth and helps your bones to grow and become strong
- Vitamin A helps heart, lungs and kidneys work efficiently, is important for normal vision and for good skin
- Vitamin C in citrus fruits, for example oranges or lemons, boosts your immune system and helps repair skin and keeps gums healthy
- B vitamins in leafy green vegetables help your body to use proteins, fats and carbohydrates more efficiently.

Minerals

Minerals, like vitamins, help your body to work properly. They are important for healthy teeth, bones, blood, muscles, skin and hair. We cannot make minerals so we have to get them through our food and fluids.

The body uses minerals to perform many different functions – from building strong bones and transmitting nerve impulses, to making hormones and maintaining a normal heartbeat.

Some examples of minerals are:

- Calcium – from milk, cheese, broccoli. It's needed for strong teeth and bones
- Iron – from meat, oily fish and eggs. It's needed for keeping blood and muscle healthy
- Potassium – from fruit and green vegetables. It regulates the level of water in our bodies, and keeps our nervous system healthy.

Fats

Fat is found in food. Some foods such as fruit and vegetables have very little fat and are called 'low-fat' foods. Other foods such as nuts, oils and butter, are high-fat foods. Our bodies need fats and oil but only in small amounts. Fat provides energy, keeps us warm and helps us to absorb certain vitamins.

Food labelled 'high in polyunsaturated' or 'monounsaturated fat' are healthier for our hearts. Fish oils help our memory. Toddlers and young children need more fats so that their brain develops properly. That is why young children should drink full-fat milk. Older children can drink low-fat milk.

Water

Water is essential for life. It makes up two-thirds of your body weight and is necessary for all of your cells and organs to work properly. Without water we would die of dehydration in a few days. You should drink water regularly. Eight cups of fluid is the recommended daily amount.

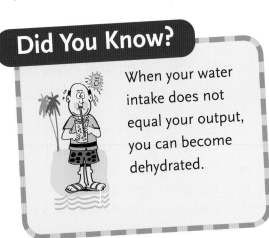

We lose fluid from our bodies constantly so it's important to replace it. Sweating, breathing and urinating are the most usual ways we lose fluids. If the weather is warm or we exercise, we lose even more fluids than normal and we need to replace them by increasing our intake of water. You can also get water by drinking juice, soup or milk.

Did You Know?

When your water intake does not equal your output, you can become dehydrated.

Supplements

If you eat a varied and balanced diet, there is normally no need to take any food supplements – you'll get everything you need from your food. The one exception to this is folic acid. All women of child-bearing age who could become pregnant should take a supplement of 400µg (micrograms) folic acid each day. This ensures the healthy development of the baby. If a woman does become pregnant, she should continue to take the supplement during the first twelve weeks of pregnancy.

Activity 4

What's in food?

Using the clues below complete this crossword. You will find all the information you need for the answers on the previous two pages.

Across

1 The Vitamin D found in this helps your bones
2 This vitamin is found in green, leafy vegetables
4 Provides energy for the body
6 Build and maintain body tissue
8 Found in grains, wheat and rice
10 You will find fat in these
11 Source of carbohydrate
12 Carbohydrates are the main source of this in the body
13 Helps digestion
15 Good source of Vitamin C

Down

1 Like vitamins, these help your body to work properly
3 This happens if you lose too much water
5 Carbohydrates are broken down into simple forms of this
7 These have almost no fat
9 Amount of glasses of liquid to be drank daily
14 Found in red meat

The Food Pyramid

The Food Pyramid shows us how to eat healthily. It is for adults, teenagers and children aged five and over. We should eat more of the foods on the bottom shelf and only dip into the foods on the the top shelf now and again, as a treat!

All age groups need to reduce foods and drinks from the top shelf, especially younger children (5–13 years). Avoiding these foods will help you to be a healthy weight. Taken in excess, these foods can be harmful.

All age groups need to follow these guidelines carefully to restrict fat, saturated fat and calories. Fats, spreads and oils are essential, but only in very small amounts.

These foods are essential for good health. Have fish at least twice a week and oily fish once a week. Pregnant and breast-feeding women should eat only one serving of tuna per week.

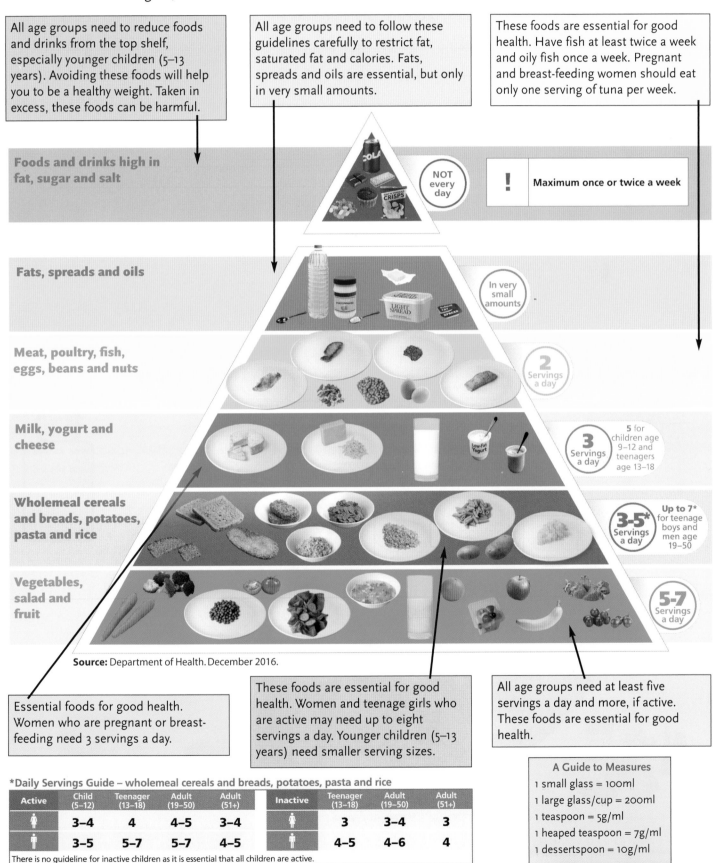

Foods and drinks high in fat, sugar and salt

NOT every day

! Maximum once or twice a week

Fats, spreads and oils

In very small amounts

Meat, poultry, fish, eggs, beans and nuts

2 Servings a day

Milk, yogurt and cheese

3 Servings a day — 5 for children age 9–12 and teenagers age 13–18

Wholemeal cereals and breads, potatoes, pasta and rice

3-5* Servings a day — Up to 7* for teenage boys and men age 19–50

Vegetables, salad and fruit

5-7 Servings a day

Source: Department of Health. December 2016.

Essential foods for good health. Women who are pregnant or breast-feeding need 3 servings a day.

These foods are essential for good health. Women and teenage girls who are active may need up to eight servings a day. Younger children (5–13 years) need smaller serving sizes.

All age groups need at least five servings a day and more, if active. These foods are essential for good health.

A Guide to Measures
1 small glass = 100ml
1 large glass/cup = 200ml
1 teaspoon = 5g/ml
1 heaped teaspoon = 7g/ml
1 dessertspoon = 10g/ml

*Daily Servings Guide – wholemeal cereals and breads, potatoes, pasta and rice

Active	Child (5–12)	Teenager (13–18)	Adult (19–50)	Adult (51+)	Inactive	Teenager (13–18)	Adult (19–50)	Adult (51+)
♀	3–4	4	4–5	3–4	♀	3	3–4	3
♂	3–5	5–7	5–7	4–5	♂	4–5	4–6	4

There is no guideline for inactive children as it is essential that all children are active.

Activity 5

Find the food!

There are many examples of the different types of food in the picture of the Food Pyramid on page 59. See if you can find at least three examples each of the foods that are sources of water, carbohydrates, proteins, fats, minerals and vitamins and write them below.

Sources of water: _____

Sources of carbohydrates: _____

Sources of proteins: _____

Sources of fats: _____

Sources of minerals: _____

Sources of vitamins: _____

The Eatwell Guide

Another way of looking at the food you eat!

Sometimes you see healthy eating illustrated by the Eatwell Guide. This is an idea that came from the European Union organisation Safefood (see www.safefood.eu).

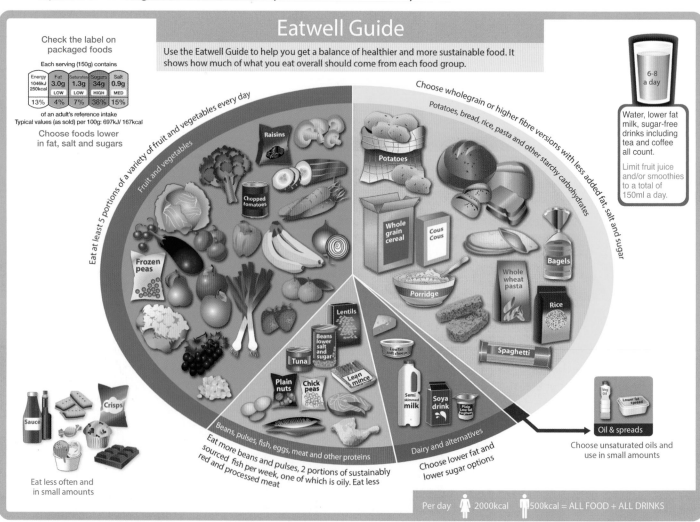

The plate is designed to make healthy eating easier. If you eat foods from each group, in the correct amounts each day, you'll get the balance of energy and nutrients you need to have good health.

Foods that are like each other sit together in the same group and can be swapped. So if you don't like potatoes you can eat rice or pasta instead. You don't have to get the balance right at every meal, but you should try to get it right over a whole day or throughout the week.

Activity 6

The eatwell challenge

On the empty eatwell plate below write the names of the foods you have had from each category in the past 24-hours. Remember to include all your meals, snacks, school lunches and so on. Use the information from the Food Pyramid to help you. Then answer the questions which follow.

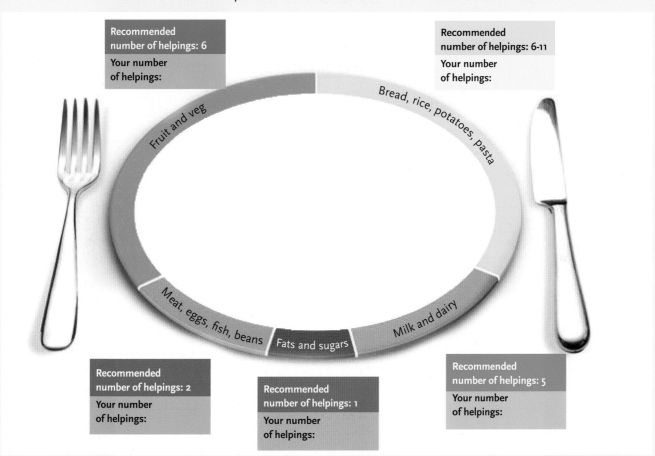

Recommended number of helpings: 6
Your number of helpings:

Recommended number of helpings: 6-11
Your number of helpings:

Fruit and veg

Bread, rice, potatoes, pasta

Meat, eggs, fish, beans

Fats and sugars

Milk and dairy

Recommended number of helpings: 2
Your number of helpings:

Recommended number of helpings: 1
Your number of helpings:

Recommended number of helpings: 5
Your number of helpings:

1 How well did your plate compare with the recommended helpings for healthy eating?

_____

2 List the areas where you need to improve.

_____

3 Write down two things you can start to do to make your diet more balanced.

_____

Changing Your Eating Habits!

Knowing what makes a healthy diet doesn't mean we eat healthily. We need to look at the unhealthy habits we have and change them.

Activity 7

Healthy eating competition

Your school is running a competition to design a healthy evening meal: starter, main course and dessert. It has to be suitable for people of your age. The meal should be exciting and tasty and must fit in with the food pyramid. Design a menu for the meal and write in your ideas below.

Menu

Think about what you have learned in these activities and complete the sentences below.

A goal that I set for myself to make my diet healthier is

To do this I need to

Somebody who can help me with this is

because

Brain food

Eating well is good for your mental, as well as your physical, health. These foods are particularly important for keeping our grey matter (brain) happy!

1. Wholegrains
2. Oily fish
3. Blueberries
4. Tomatoes
5. B6, B12 and folic acid
6. Blackcurrants
7. Pumpkin seeds
8. Broccoli
9. Sage
10. Nuts

Food Labelling

Under EU law, food labelling must be used to tell consumers everything that is in pre-packaged food. The most important rule of labelling is that the label is clear and easy to read so that the customer can check the food value per 100g and per serving. Be careful if you are using the 'per serving' figures on the food label to work out what you are eating as many of us take much larger servings than the ones stated on food labels!

Learning how to compare food labels correctly can be the difference between you choosing healthy food to eat or you having empty calories (calories from food that has no nutrients) in your diet.

The first thing we need to look at is product size. Are the two things you are comparing the same weight? Usually they are not so it's best to read the **100g** column on the food label and look at the amount of calories, fat, fibre and sugar listed on it.

Reading the food label

Ingredients are listed in order from most to least in quantity.

This is the total of both sugar and starch.

Look for low fat content per 100g. Choose foods with less than 10g fat per 100g. Choose milks and yoghurts with less than 2g fat per 100g.

Look for the product with more fibre per 100g (more than 8g fibre per 100g for breakfast cereals).

Use the 100g column for the easiest comparison.

Look for foods with much more total carbohydrates than sugars alone.

Look for no more than 120mg sodium per 100g food or no more than 0.3% sodium per 100g.

Typical values	100g contains	45g serving contains
Energy	1570kJ 375kcal	710kJ 170kcal
Protein	10.3g	4.6g
Carbohydrate	73.8g	33.2g
of which sugars	15.0g	6.8g
Fat	2.0g	0.9g
of which saturates	0.3g	0.1g
Fibre‡‡	8.2g	3.7g
Sodium	0.2g	0.1g
Salt equivalent	0.6g	0.3g

...RDA) and adding a handful of fruit will count as one of your 5-a-Day.

‡‡Fibre has been determined by AOA...
for guideline dai...

What are you eating?

Do you really know what you are eating? Look at the food labels on page 65. There are a number of differences between them. You need to look out for:

- Is the information per serving or per 100g? Be aware of the differences!

- Total calories per serving

- Total sugar (grams) per serving

- Total fat (grams) per serving

- Amount of salt (sodium) per serving

- Percentage (%) daily value of an ingredient, this is the amount that the product contains compared with the Guidance Daily Amount (GDA).

Nutrition Facts

Almonds

Serving Size 100g/3.5oz

Amount	% Daily Value
Calories 580	
Calories from Fat 440	
Total Fat 51 g	78%
Saturated Fat 4 g	20%
Trans Fat 0 g	
Cholesterol 0 mg	0%
Sodium 1 mg	1%
Carbohydrate 20 g	7%
Fiber 12 g	48%
Sugars 5 g	
Protein 21 g	
Vitamin A	0%
Vitamin C	0%
Calcium	27%
Iron	25%

Activity 8

Know your label!

<table>
<tr><th colspan="3" style="text-align:center">Label A Crispy Pops</th></tr>
<tr><th colspan="3" style="text-align:center">NUTRITIONAL INFORMATION</th></tr>
</table>

	Typical value per 100g	Typical value per 30g serving
ENERGY	1530kJ 340kcal	459kJ 102kcal
FAT of which saturates	2.3g 0.9g	0.6g 0.2g
CARBOHYDRATE of which sugars	79g 28g	23g 8g
FIBRE	1g	0.3g
PROTEIN	4.2g	1.2g
SALT	0.6g	0.18g

VITAMINS:		(%NRV)		(%NRV)
VITAMIN D	4.2µg	(83)	1.3µg	(25)
THIAMIN (B₁)	0.91mg	(83)	0.28mg	(25)
RIBOFLAVIN (B₂)	1.2mg	(83)	0.35mg	(25)
NIACIN	12.9mg	(78)	3.9mg	(25)
VITAMIN (B₆)	1.2mg	(83)	0.35mg	(25)
FOLIC ACID	166µg	(83)	50.0µg	(25)
VITAMIN (B₁₂)	2.1µg	(83)	0.63µg	(25)
MINERALS:				
CALCIUM	456mg	(57)	136mg	(17)
IRON	8.0mg	(57)	2.4mg	(17)

(%NRV) = % Nutrient Reference Value
REFERENCE INTAKES (RIs)

494Kj 117kcal — This is the amount of energy in one bowl.

6% — This is the percentage of your daily energy allowance that one bowl will provide.

<table>
<tr><th colspan="4" style="text-align:center">Label B Porridge</th></tr>
<tr><th colspan="4" style="text-align:center">NUTRITIONAL INFORMATION</th></tr>
</table>

Typical values	per 100g	per 40g serving (with water)	Reference Intake**
Energy	1409kJ 334kcal	563kJ 92kcal	8400kJ 2000kcal
Fat of which saturates	5.2g 0.9g	2.1g 0.3g	63g 18g
Carbohydrate of which sugars	58g 0.8g	23g 0.4g	234g 81g
Fibre	7.5g	3g	
Protein	10g	4g	45g
Salt	<0.01g	<0.01g	5.5g
Iron	3.2mg (23% NRV***)	1.3mg (10% NRV)	
Thiamin (B₁)	0.32mg (30% NRV)	0.13mg (12% NRV)	

**Reference Intake of an average adult (8400kJ/2000kcal)

*** Nutrient Reference Value

Look at the labels A and B above and answer the questions below.

1. Which has the highest amount of protein per serving? _____

2. Which has the lowest fat content per serving? _____

3. Which would be healthiest if you were watching your salt intake? _____

4. How different are the serving sizes? _____

5. Which do you think would be healthiest, and why? _____

_____

6. Which has the lowest amount of sugar per 100g? _____

Did You Know?

Eating too much salt (sodium) is not good for your health. It can lead to raised blood pressure, which triples your chances of developing heart disease and having a stroke. The recommended amount of salt for children is 3–5g a day. Pepper can be used instead of salt to flavour food. About 80 per cent of the salt that you eat is hidden in everyday foods. These include processed meats, bacon, sausages, puddings, ready-made meals and sauces. Packet soups, stock cubes, gravy granules and some breakfast cereals and breads are also high in salt, as are salty snacks from the top shelf of the food pyramid. Eat less of these high salt foods and remember to check the label for salt content before you eat anything.

Activity

9 Healthy eating

Fill in the blanks in the text below. Try to do it without help first by covering the words listed in the word bank on page 67. However, they are there if you get stuck and need them!

Limit foods and drinks from the _____ Shelf of the Food Pyramid as these are high in fat, _____ and salt. Always read the nutrition label – check for high levels of fat, sugar and salt. Ready-meals and takeaways tend to be high in _____ and should not be eaten regularly. Eat _____ or more of different coloured fruit and vegetables every day. Eat more fish; it's a good source of _____, as well as containing important vitamins and minerals. Try to eat oily fish at least once a week, for example _____. Try other flavourings instead of _____ such as herbs, spices, pepper, garlic or lemon juice.

Adults need about _____ glasses of fluid every day. You need more if you are active. Children and teenagers need to drink regularly throughout the day. _____ is the best fluid. Always make time to have a good _____ – people who eat breakfast are more likely to be a healthy weight. If you eat a healthy, balanced diet, you should not need to take _____, unless you are advised to do so by your doctor. If you are overweight, consider the quantity of foods you eat from all the shelves of the Food Pyramid, with the exception of _____.

Nutrition Facts

Apple, raw
Serving Size 100g/3.5oz

Amount	
	% Daily Value
Calories 55	
Calories from Fat 1	
Total Fat 0.3 g	
Saturated Fat 0 g	1%
Trans Fat 0 g	0%
Cholesterol 0 mg	
Sodium 0 mg	0%
Carbohydrate 15 g	0%
Fiber 3 g	6%
Sugars 10 g	11%
Protein 0.2 g	
Vitamin A	
Vitamin C	1%
Calcium	8%
Iron	1%
	1%

Word Bank

protein, fruit and vegetables, salt, sugar, fat and salt, food supplements, breakfast, salmon, trout and mackerel, five, top, eight, water

Learning Log

The three important facts that I must look for on food labels are:

1 _____

_____

2 _____

_____

3 _____

_____

_____

Rest and Physical Activity

Sleep

Having enough sleep and rest is essential in order to stay healthy and work efficiently. During sleep:

- The wear and tear of the day is repaired
- The body rebuilds its energy levels
- The body mends itself, which helps protect against illness and disease
- The brain recharges during sleep, which results in better concentration.

Did You Know?

A number of studies indicate that children who don't get enough sleep are prone to behavioural problems. In 2009 Finnish researchers found that children who slept fewer than 7.7 hours a night were more prone to hyperactivity, restlessness, impulsiveness and lack of concentration.

Activity 10

Sleep cycle

Fill in the chart showing how many hours you sleep each night, and what you were doing before you went to sleep. Indicate also how well you slept (easy to get to sleep, a restless sleep etc.). Can you see any links?

Nights	Hours asleep	Quality of your sleep	What did you do before you went to sleep?
Monday			
Tuesday			
Wednesday			
Thursday			
Friday			
Saturday			
Sunday			
Total hours slept			

Tips for a good sleep

- Get into a routine, go to bed at the same time each night
- Avoid stimulants such as sweets, tea or coffee at night
- Avoid food that might cause you to sleep uneasily
- Avoid vigorous exercise before you go to bed
- Make sure your room is dark and quiet (noise is the enemy of sleep!)
- Don't have your room too warm. Fresh air helps you sleep
- Using lavender drops on your pillow or a sachet of lavender seeds beside your pillow can help you sleep
- Listen to relaxing music or read for a while before going to sleep
- Never fall asleep watching TV or listening to the radio or music on your phone
- Keep electronic gadgets away from your bed. Turn off TVs, radios, mobile phones and computers.

Study the 'Tips for a good sleep' and see what changes you can make to ensure that you have a good sleep every night!

Did You Know?

The amount of sleep required is different for each person.

Q. How much sleep does your body need?

A. Listen to your body! It will tell you how much sleep you need. Usually teenagers need between eight and eleven hours a night. Not having enough sleep results in you becoming tired and irritable and finding it hard to learn and remember. You also catch colds and other infections more easily.

LEARNING LOG

Two changes I will make so that I have a good night's sleep are:

1

2

Physical Activity

If you exercise regularly, at least 60 minutes every day, it can have loads of benefits including:

- Reducing the risk of heart disease
- Helping you to get a good night's sleep
- Keeping your weight in check
- Making you feel happier
- Reducing your stress levels
- Helping you to meet people and be part of a group
- Making studying easier
- Helping you to learn leadership qualities and team spirit.

Physical exercise is free and is one of the best things you can do for your overall health and wellbeing.

KEY WORDS

Physical activity

Any body movement that works your muscles and requires more energy than resting. Walking, running, dancing, swimming, yoga and gardening are a few examples of physical activity. Physical activity generally refers to any movement that enhances your health.

Activity 11 — Getting active

Read the list of the benefits of physical activity on the previous page and see if you can add two or three benefits to it.

_____

_____

_____

Activity 12 — Physical activity and me!

Before deciding how to improve your level of physical activity think about what you are doing now. Look at the four statements below and mark where you are on the 'Like me – Not like me' line. You may be at either end or somewhere in the middle.

1. I enjoy being physically active and take part in a variety of activities at least five days a week.

   Like me _____ Not like me

2. I used to be more physically active but have less time now. I try to exercise at least three days a week, but it doesn't always work out!

   Like me _____ Not like me

3. I am not very physically active but would like to become more involved as I know it is good for me. How do I start?

   Like me _____ Not like me

4. I am not at all physically active and have never enjoyed sports or other exercise. I enjoy playing computer games or listening to music much more.

   Like me _____ Not like me

Did You Know?

Sports/energy drinks are high in sugar and energy but people following the guidelines for regular physical activity, who are exercising at least 60 minutes most days of the week, don't need these drinks. In fact, having these extra 'empty' calories can undo the benefits of physical activity in helping to maintain a healthy weight. (See www.healthpromotion.ie)

Activity 13

Physical Activity Pyramid

Now that you have thought about your own level of physical activity let's look at how you can get more involved in some type of exercise. Study the Physical Activity Pyramid. It shows the kinds of activities you need to do, and the number of times you need to do them per week if you want to be physically fit. In the circles below write the number of times each week you get involved in each of the four levels of physical activity. Then answer the two questions.

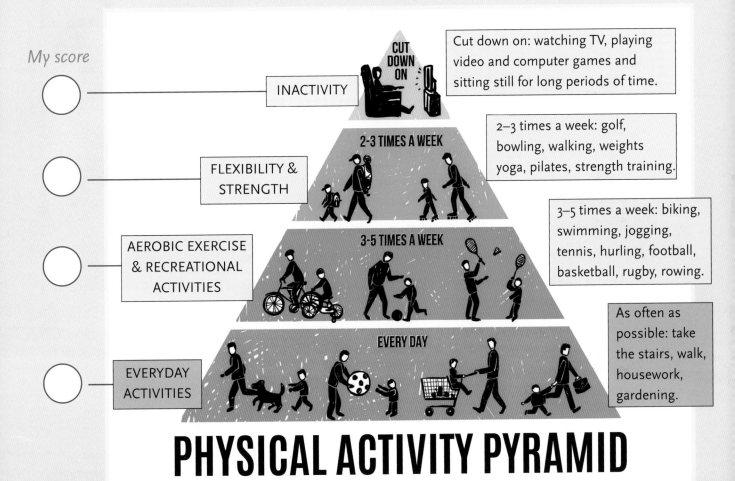

My score

INACTIVITY

Cut down on: watching TV, playing video and computer games and sitting still for long periods of time.

FLEXIBILITY & STRENGTH

2–3 times a week: golf, bowling, walking, weights yoga, pilates, strength training.

AEROBIC EXERCISE & RECREATIONAL ACTIVITIES

3–5 times a week: biking, swimming, jogging, tennis, hurling, football, basketball, rugby, rowing.

As often as possible: take the stairs, walk, housework, gardening.

EVERYDAY ACTIVITIES

PHYSICAL ACTIVITY PYRAMID

1 Are you doing as much physical activity as you should be?

_____

2 If not, which level do you need to focus most on?

_____

Experts recommend that young people do at least 60 minutes of moderate and vigorous physical activity every day. If you want, this can be made up of six bursts of activity which are at least ten minutes long each time.

Daily Exercise and Young People

The figures in the table show the percentage of children who get the recommended level of physical activity every day – a minimum of 60 minutes.

Age	Boys	Girls
10–11 years	42%	31%
12–14 years	31%	18%
15–17 years	20%	9%

Percentage rate of achievement of daily physical activity.
Figures taken from HBSC 2014

Physical activity plan

Now you know what you should be doing! Let's draw up a plan (see below), but first here are some tips:

- Decide what you want to do and write it in your weekly diary or in the table below. You are more likely to stick to your plan if you write it down!

- Set yourself a goal. Decide on what you will do and for how long (use the pyramid as a guide).

- Track your progress. Mark off in your diary when you completed the activity.

- Take part in different activities if you are bored with just one.

- Find a 'buddy' to support you along the way. Remember you will also have to support your 'buddy'.

- Choose a physical activity that you enjoy.

Activity 14 · Activity planner

Activity	Pyramid level activity	Goal	Recommended times	How I did
Fast walk to school (25 mins) instead of taking the bus	Level 2 aerobic activity	To do this two mornings a week (to start!)	At least 20 mins, three times a week	

LEARNING LOG

Two changes I will make to improve my level of physical activity are:

1

2

Useful Websites

www.safefood.eu – interesting facts on the Eatwell Guide and healthy eating

www.nourishinteractive.com – nutrition facts and recipes

www.kidshealth.org – use this website to look up useful facts on nutrition

www.croi.ie – look up useful facts on how to have a healthy heart and get physically active

www.getirelandactive.ie – great tips for how to get active

Assessment – Check your learning

Using the Useful Websites above and any others you can find, create a slide show, poster or a speech for your classmates on 'The Importance of Diet and Physical Activity for Physical, Social and Mental Wellbeing'.

Your presentation should include recommendations and practical ideas for improving the diet and level of physical activity among first-year students. Save your presentation to your e-folder or SPHE folder.

Review of Unit 1: *Being Healthy*

1 In this unit I learned about _____

_____

_____

2 I think that this will help me when _____

_____

_____

3 In this unit I liked _____

_____

_____

4 In this unit I did not like _____

_____

_____

5 I would like to find out more about _____

_____

_____

6 This unit links with (name another unit in SPHE or another subject) _____

_____

_____

UNIT 2 — Substance Use

Learning Outcomes:

This unit helps you to:

1. Explore the nature and use of drugs in modern life ○

2. Understand the role and safe use of medicines and how to store and dispose of them ○

3. Identify and explain the personal, social and legal consequences of smoking and misusing alcohol and solvents ○

4. Become familiar with the role of help agencies that deal with substance abuse ○

5. Understand what peer pressure is and the role it plays in young people smoking and drinking alcohol ○

6. Practise strategies for dealing with peer pressure. ○

(Tick each topic off as you complete it.)

Medicines and Drugs in Our Lives

Drugs and medicines play an important part in our lives, for example they help us to manage pain and fight infection, but they can sometimes be misused. In this unit we will study the most common drugs in our day-to-day lives – medicines; solvents such as glue, petrol or nail polish; alcohol; tobacco – and we will also look at illegal drugs such as cannabis, cocaine and ecstasy.

KEY WORDS

Drug
Drug misuse
Drug addiction
Alcohol
Standard drinks/
Units of alcohol
Solvents/Solvent abuse
Smoking
E-cigarettes
Peer pressure
Self-esteem

Medicines

People use medicines when they are ill, to help them get better and to prevent disease.

There are three types of medicine:

- **Prescription medicines**: Medication that is prescribed by a doctor.

- **Over the counter (OTC) medicine:** Medication that we can buy in the supermarket or in a pharmacy without having a prescription, including some painkillers and cream for minor burns.

- **Complementary and alternative medicine (CAM):** The definition of what is a complementary or alternative medicine changes. To put it simply, these are medicines or therapies which claim to have the healing effects of regular medicine but are not based on strict scientific testing and evidence. Examples include using herbs, special diets, massage, vitamin mixtures, meditation and energy fields to treat illnesses. If these are used along with regular medicines they are called complementary medicines, but if they are used instead of regular medicines they are called alternative medicines.

Many doctors encourage the use of complementary medicine, for example acupuncture (a traditional Chinese complementary medicine, using needles) or special diets, to help with the treatment for some illnesses.

KEY WORDS

Drug

A chemical that causes changes in the way our body works mentally, physically or emotionally. Drugs in daily life include many medicines as well as substances we may not normally think of as drugs such as tea, coffee, alcohol, solvents and tobacco.

REMEMBER

Never take medication that was prescribed for someone else! When doctors prescribe medicines they take into account the patient's medical history, physical condition, allergies and other factors before deciding what medication is suitable for that patient only.

Storing medicines

All medicines need to be stored safely as medication can be dangerous in the home, particularly to young children or other vulnerable people. Most medicines should be stored in a cool, dry, locked cupboard (unless stated otherwise on the label).

Using medicines without supervision may cause poisoning or other nasty side effects.

1 A healthy house

Look at the image of the house below and circle the places in each room where medicines, cleaning agents (toilet cleaners, bleach, sink unblockers), solvents (glue, paint-thinners, nail polish remover), poisons (rat poison, weedkiller, barbecue-lighter fluid), cigarettes and alcohol might be found.

1 Do you think these are good places to store these materials? Why/why not?

_____

_____

_____

_____

📰 **PowerPoint**

2 On your own, or with other students, create an information leaflet or poster for house owners to advise them on safe ways to store these materials in their homes.

Disposal of medicines

Apart from making sure that medicines are stored properly, clearing out the medicine cabinet and safely disposing of medicines is something that should be done regularly, as medicines need to be disposed of properly when they are out of date. Prescribed and OTC medicines will have an expiry date on the container. It is usually written as something like 'Exp: 05/2023' – in this case the medicine is safe to use until the end of May 2023.

Something you can do to make your home safer is to ask a parent or guardian to help you to check all the dates on any medicines. If you find any that are out of date, you and your parent should return them to any pharmacy. Medicines, whether they are out of date or not, should never be flushed down the toilet or washed down the sink as they can damage the environment and be harmful to animals.

KEY WORDS

Drug misuse/drug addiction
The use of any drug, legal or illegal, which damages some aspect of your life.

Drug misuse/drug addiction

Sometimes when we think of people having a drug problem we think only of illegal drugs such as cannabis, cocaine, ecstasy or heroin. But drug addiction can also include the use of legal drugs such as alcohol, tobacco, prescription and OTC medicines, as well as the incorrect use of solvents, for example glue-sniffing.

LEARNING LOG

I learned three new things about medicines and drugs:

1 _____

2 _____

3 _____

Alcohol

Alcohol is a depressant. This means it slows down the messages going from the brain to the rest of the body, which changes the way a person feels, thinks, hears, sees and moves.

Did You Know?

You must be over 18 years of age to buy alcohol in Ireland. It is illegal to sell alcohol to, or to buy alcohol for, anyone under 18.

KEY WORDS

Alcohol
A mood altering drink. The main active ingredient is a chemical called ethanol, which is made by fermenting sugar or yeast.

Alcohol fact sheet

Alcohol is measured by a standard drink (SD). One unit of alcohol contains 10g of pure alcohol. The recommended weekly level for low-risk drinking for adults is:

Women	Men
Maximum: Eleven standard drinks per week.	Maximum: Seventeen standard drinks per week.
No more than three drinks per day with at least two alcohol-free days per week.	No more than four drinks per day, with at least two alcohol-free days per week.

1 Standard Drink (SD) contains 10g of pure alcohol

1SD = Half pint beer/stout/ale/cider **or** Pub measure spirit **or** Small glass wine **or** Alcopop (275ml bottle)

Some drinks are more than one Standard Drink 10g of pure alcohol

2SD Pint beer/stout/ale

2SD Double pub measure spirit

2SD Pint cider

2SD Quarter bottle wine

2SD Large can beer

Note: Spirits refer to drinks such as vodka, gin, whiskey, rum, etc. A small glass of wine is 125ml. There are 750ml in a regular bottle of wine.

Did You Know?

Every year, in Ireland 30 per cent of unnatural deaths are alcohol-related.

Useful Websites

www.drugs.ie – you can take a quick Alcohol Fact quiz

Activity 2
Alcohol quiz/walking debate

Let's check how much you already know about alcohol – the most commonly used drug in Irish society. Working in groups, read the twelve statements below and decide if each is True or False and give a reason for your choice in one short sentence. You can use the websites on page 89 to help you.

	Statement	True/False	Reason
1	Alcohol is a stimulant – it wakes you up.		
2	Alcohol affects women more than men.		
3	It is impossible to tell how much alcohol is in a bottle or a drink.		
4	A half pint of beer, a glass of wine and a shot of spirits all contain the same amount of alcohol.		
5	Every night in Ireland 1,000 hospital beds are occupied by people admitted for alcohol-related reasons.		
6	In Ireland you can legally buy alcohol in off-licences at 16 years of age.		
7	Binge drinking is defined as drinking at least six units of alcohol in one sitting.		
8	Ireland was ranked tenth out of 194 countries for binge drinking, just behind Britain.		
9	Alcohol increases people's risk of developing more than 200 diseases, including several forms of cancer.		
10	Drinking black coffee, water or having a cold shower helps someone to sober up.		
11	There are the same amount of deaths due to alcohol in Ireland each year as there are deaths due to all other drugs combined.		
12	An estimated €527 million is lost each year in Ireland due to alcohol-related work place accidents and sick days.		

Your teacher will give you the correct answers.

 PowerPoint

What information surprised you the most from this quiz?

_____

_____

_____

Some facts about alcohol

- Alcohol is a legal drug

- Alcohol is the most misused drug in Ireland

- The effects of alcohol on the body may last several hours

- Drinking alcohol can lead to feelings of sadness and depression

- Binge drinking is when you have five drinks or more at one time

- If you begin drinking at thirteen you are four times more likely to have health problems when you are twenty-four than those who start drinking at twenty-one

- Regular drinking can lead to dependence or addiction

- Drinking alcohol as a teenager can damage your memory permanently

- Heavy drinking can result in increased risk of stroke, heart disease, stomach problems and liver disease

- People who drink too much hurt not only themselves, but also their families and friends

- About 10 per cent of those who drink become addicted to alcohol

- It is illegal for anyone under the age of eighteen to buy alcohol in Ireland.

Activity

3 | Alcohol fact file

Read the facts about alcohol above and answer the questions below.

1 The fact that surprised me the most was _____

because _____

2 The fact that surprised me the least was _____

because _____

3 The fact that I think is most important is _____

because _____

Effects of alcohol on the body

Stages of Intoxication

Happy   Elated   Confused   Stupor   Coma

← *Amount of alcohol consumed* →

Brain

Alcohol acts as a depressant and can make the drinker feel happy for a little while, but that's followed by a depressing low. Long-term drinking can kill off brain cells and lead to memory loss and mental health problems.

Hair

Alcohol lowers the amount of some essential minerals in the body, including zinc. Too little zinc causes hair loss.

Head

After a few drinks, it can be easy for someone to 'lose the head' or lose control. Their judgement is affected too. They might make a fool of themselves, get into trouble, cause an accident or do something they regret later. Alcohol draws water out of the brain. So, as the body starts to metabolise the alcohol, the drinker may feel dizzy and end up with a throbbing headache if they drink too much.

Eyes

Too much alcohol dilates blood vessels in the eyes, so they can look red and 'bloodshot'. Vision becomes blurred, and distances and speeds get harder to judge and result in distorted vision. Many road accidents involve drivers or pedestrians who have alcohol in their blood.

Too much alcohol also suppresses REM (Rapid Eye Movement) sleep. It's the most important phase of sleep so drinking can ruin your chance of a good night's rest.

Throat

Bleeding ulcers.

Speech

Too much alcohol can cause people to say things which are hurtful, cause arguments or get them into trouble. It can also lead to slurred speech.

Armpits

One of the ways the body gets rid of alcohol is as a smelly body odour.

Waist

Although alcohol is fat free, it is very high in calories and increases your appetite, so it can lead to weight gain.

Heart

Drinking large quantities of alcohol causes high blood pressure, heart disease and abnormal heart rhythms.

Skin

Too much alcohol dehydrates the body and can damage your skin and complexion. It can also cause ugly veins on your nose and cheeks.

Reproductive organs

Drinking too much alcohol can cause impotence in men and may delay periods and affect fertility in women. As alcohol crosses from the mother's bloodstream to the unborn baby, you should not drink alcohol at all if you are pregnant.

Legs

Alcohol affects co-ordination which leads to difficulty in walking a straight line so even crossing the road can be dangerous.

Liver

Long-term heavy drinking kills liver cells, leading to a disease called 'cirrhosis' (*sir-o-sis*). It's a 'silent' disease – symptoms may not be noticeable until the disease is advanced. Long-term excessive drinking can also lead to liver cancer.

Stomach

Alcohol can cause stomach ulcers or cancer and, as it is toxic, too much can cause vomiting.

 **PowerPoint**

Which effect of alcohol on the body did you find most surprising?

Which effect of alcohol on the body do you think is the most serious? Why?

Parents' drinking

Children of all ages suffer when a parent has a problem with drinking. One in eleven children in Ireland say their lives are negatively affected by a parent's drinking.

Children are never to blame when a parent has a drink problem.

You didn't **cause** it.

You can't **control** it.

You can't **cure** it.

3Cs

If you are a young person affected by a parent's drinking please visit www.DrinkHelp.ie, www.drugs.ie or www.barnardos.ie for information, advice and details of support services. Consider talking to an adult or a relative (grandparent, aunt) you trust or to the school counsellor.

Solvents

A person who has inhaled solvents behaves like someone who is drunk. This behaviour can result in accidents or serious injury.

Solvents also slow down the different systems in the body and can result in the user becoming unconscious, which can lead to death.

Below are some other effects of solvent abuse:

- Nausea (feeling sick) may lead to choking as a result of vomiting

- Inhaling solvents may cause a rash in the nose or mouth and damage the lining of the nose

- Regular solvent abuse can cause brain damage due to the lack of oxygen to the brain

- Death from heart failure can result from damage to the heart muscle

- Memory loss and coma may occur from the effects of the solvents on the brain

- Death from lung failure (not being able to breathe) may result from the freezing effect of some solvents (aerosols) in the airways.

Activity 4

Solvents quiz

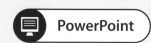 PowerPoint

Answer true (T) or false (F) to these statements. Your teacher will go through the correct answers later.

	Statements	True/False
1	Inhaling solvents is illegal.	
2	Solvent abuse can cause sudden death.	
3	It is illegal to sell solvents.	
4	Solvent abuse is a form of drug-taking.	
5	Short-term abuse of solvents can cause breathing difficulties and heart problems.	
6	Solvent abuse puts you at risk of developing violent behaviour.	
7	Regular abuse of solvents can lead to addiction.	
8	You are not at risk of death the first time you inhale solvents.	
9	Teenagers buying solvents in a shop can be refused, if the shopkeeper suspects that they are buying them to inhale.	
10	Solvents include deodorants, air fresheners and lighter fuels.	

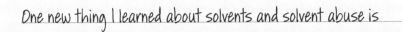

One new thing I learned about solvents and solvent abuse is

If I knew my friend was abusing solvents I would get help for her/him by

Smoking

Smoking is the inhalation of the smoke from burning tobacco. It occurs mostly in three forms: cigarettes, pipes and cigars. Read these facts and use them to answer the smoking quiz in Activity 5 on page 86.

Facts about smoking

- Regular smoking as a teenager does more damage than smoking later in life
- Cigarettes are responsible for 30 per cent of all cancer deaths, and 20 per cent of all deaths from heart disease and strokes. Also 80 per cent of all chronic lung disease is caused by smoking
- 6,000 deaths each year in Ireland are directly related to smoking.

- Nicotine is more addictive than heroin, cocaine, cannabis, alcohol and caffeine
- It is illegal to sell cigarettes to anyone under 18 years of age
- The law says that we must be protected from passive smoke (inhaling other people's smoke) while at school, work, shopping, in cinemas, theatres, restaurants and bars.

- Sidestream smoke contains 270 per cent more nicotine and 100 times more carcinogenic (cancer causing) compounds than mainstream smoke
- Sidestream smoke contains 70 per cent more tar than mainstream smoke and 250 per cent more carbon monoxide (a poisonous gas)
- Sidestream smoke is what we inhale through passive smoking. It is not filtered.

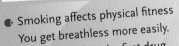

- Smoking affects physical fitness You get breathless more easily.
- Tobacco is often the first drug used by young people who use alcohol, cannabis and other drugs
- Adolescent smokers are 2.5 times more likely to have a cough with phlegm or blood than non-smokers.

More facts about smoking

- Each cigarette smoked by a regular smoker shortens his/her life by 5.5 minutes
- Cigarettes contain 4,000 different chemicals
- Children of cigarette smokers tend to be smaller and develop less well intellectually (their ability to think and reason) and emotionally than children born to non-smokers.

- It is illegal to sell cigarettes in packs of fewer than twenty
- If you smoke ten cigarettes a day there is a three- to ten-fold increase in the risk of getting a tumour (cancerous growth)
- Mainstream smoke is the smoke that is inhaled from smoking a cigarette. It is usually filtered.

- When we inhale tobacco smoke our lungs retain all of the carbon monoxide, 90 per cent of the nicotine and 70 per cent of the tar in the smoke
- Tobacco is available as cigarettes, loose tobacco, cigars and pipe tobacco.

KEY WORDS

E-cigarettes

Electronic cigarettes are battery-powered and operate using a cartridge filled with nicotine and water. They emit a vapour which is free of the harmful substances usually found in traditional cigarettes, such as tar, so they are viewed by many people as a less harmful substitute. They do, however, contain nicotine which is extremely addictive.

Activity

5 Smoking quiz

Read all of the questions before you start to answer any of them. This will make them easier and faster to answer.

1. The principal toxin (poison) in tobacco is called _____

2. Nicotine is less addictive than heroin: true or false? _____

3. The smoke we inhale from passive smoking is called _____

4. How many deaths in Ireland each year are directly related to cigarette smoking?

   600 ☐   4,250 ☐   6,000 ☐

5. A regular smoker who smokes twenty cigarettes a day is shortening their life by how many minutes per day?

   5.5 minutes ☐   60 minutes ☐   110 minutes ☐

6. Someone who smokes ten cigarettes a day is between three to ten times more likely to develop what? _____

7. What risks to children's health are caused by passive smoking? _____
   _____

8. What percentage of the tar inhaled in cigarette smoke stays in the lungs? _____

9. How many chemicals are there in tobacco smoke? _____

Effects of smoking on the body

Hair smells of smoke

Teeth become discoloured and yellow

Cancers of throat and mouth

Lung infections, emphysema (breathing difficulties), strokes, bronchitis, tumours and cancers; get short of breath affecting physical fitness

Damage to unborn baby; low birth weight, increased risk of babies being born dead or dying shortly after birth

Bad breath

Yellow staining of fingers; nasty smell of smoke from hands

Heart disease, heart attacks, bad circulation; heart has to beat two to five times faster than the heart of someone who doesn't smoke

Increased chances of infertility (being unable to conceive a child)

LEARNING LOG

Two facts that struck me most were:

1

2

Assessment – Check your learning

Make an anti-smoking poster, video or PowerPoint presentation for teenagers. Give it a catchy title and make it as interesting as possible. You can save it in either your SPHE folder or your e-folder.

Problems of Drug Misuse

On page 78 you learned that drug misuse means using any drug in a way that is damaging.

If you misuse drugs or become addicted to drugs – when you *have* to have the drink, cigarette or drug – it can cause a whole lot of problems in every area of your life and in the lives of everyone around you. Look at the poster below to see what some of those problems might be.

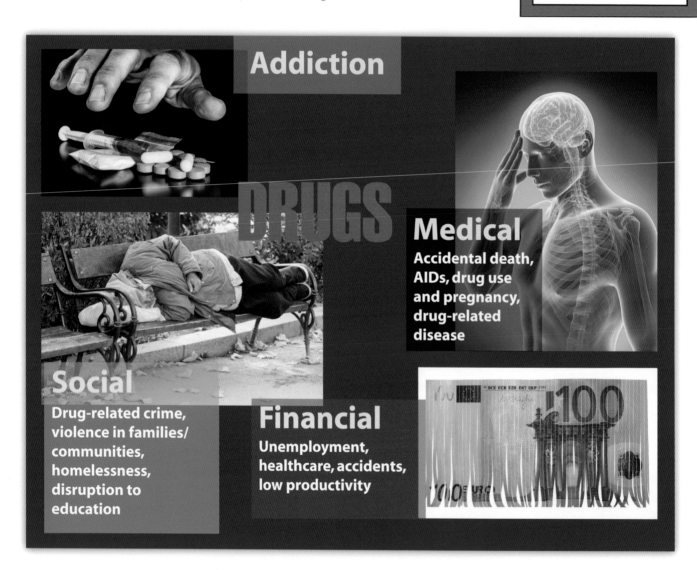

Addiction

DRUGS

Medical
Accidental death, AIDs, drug use and pregnancy, drug-related disease

Social
Drug-related crime, violence in families/communities, homelessness, disruption to education

Financial
Unemployment, healthcare, accidents, low productivity

Assessment – Check your learning

In a small group take one of the problems associated with drug misuse from the poster above. Research it using the websites on the next page and prepare a slide presentation of your findings. Remember to include facts and figures in your report. One or two slides are enough, as all of the slides from the other groups will be added together to give an overall view of the results of drug misuse.

Useful Websites

www.drugs.ie

www.alcoholireland.ie

www.yourdrinking.ie

www.abovetheinfluence.com

www.drinkaware.ie

Peer Pressure

Gavin's Story

Gavin had spent a lot of time translating sentences into French for last night's homework. Just before class, his friends Rob and Jack told him they hadn't done it and they were going to tell the teacher it was too difficult.

'I got it done,' Gavin said lamely.

'Well, say you couldn't do it either or we'll get in trouble.'

When Ms Ferris asked if anybody had done the translation, Gavin stayed silent. He was furious that he had done all that work for nothing. Now Ms Ferris would think that he couldn't do the exercise, but he knew that it wasn't worth it to go against the others.

Welcome to **peer pressure**! A peer is someone who belongs to the same age group or social group as you.

When you were young, your parents decided most things for you: what you ate, what you wore, where you went to school, who you played with. As you got older, you began to make your own decisions about these things.

In making these decisions, you are influenced by many factors: advertising, your parents and experiences, and by your friends, classmates and other people of your age (your peers).

Peer pressure happens when we do something we normally wouldn't do; or, because of the influence of people our age, we don't behave as we normally would.

All groups are affected by peer pressure. For example, adults buy four-wheel drive jeeps, even though they live in areas where these are unnecessary. And though they might disapprove, some adults give money for Communions and Confirmations because it is expected of them.

> ### KEY WORDS
>
> **Peer pressure**
>
> When your peers put pressure on you to behave in a way that they want you to behave or in the same way as they do. For example, if everyone in your group of friends smokes, peer pressure might make you start smoking as well.

Peer pressure is not always a bad thing; in fact, it is often a good thing. We study harder if our friends take school seriously. We wash and keep clean because our friends expect us to. We have good manners because it is the norm in our group. However, sometimes we do things to fit in, although we know they are wrong, for example shoplifting, bullying, lying, smoking and drinking.

Where does peer pressure come from?

Peer pressure can come directly from others telling you what to do, or encouraging you to, for example, smoke a cigarette or have a drink.

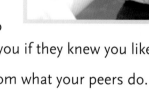

Peer pressure can also come indirectly. This is when nothing is said, but you know what is expected (remember the Confirmation money).

Sometimes peer pressure comes from you. You might stop listening to a certain kind of music because you think your friends would laugh at you if they knew you liked it.

You have to be a strong person to do your own thing if it is different from what your peers do. In this way, peer pressure is linked to self-esteem.

How we are as males and females (our sexuality) is influenced by the expectations and comments of our friends. What we wear, our hobbies, our attitude to our families and our sexual behaviour are all influenced by what we believe others think of us.

Activity

6 Your story

After reading Gavin's story and about where peer pressure comes from, write you own story to explain peer pressure.

Effects of peer pressure

Some of the ways in which young people may be affected by peer pressure are:

- How hard they work at school
- The clothes they wear
- Who they hang around with
- Whether or not they drink or do drugs
- The decision to have a boyfriend/girlfriend
- The way they speak or their accent.

KEY WORDS

Self-esteem

The word esteem has to do with how much you value something. So self-esteem refers to how much you value yourself; how worthwhile and capable you feel.

Activity 7

Sources of pressure for young people

In pairs or groups, think of all of the areas where people of your age group can feel peer pressure:

- Pressure to do what . . . ?
- To act which way . . . ?
- Pressure from whom . . . ?
- Are the pressures on boys and girls different?

Write all of these pressures on the top of the picture. Underneath the picture write all of the things that you feel would help you to deal with peer pressure. Compare what your group has written with the rest of the groups in your class and add any new suggestions.

Types of peer pressure

How to deal with peer pressure

Why is peer pressure difficult to resist?

- We want to fit in and be like the people we admire

- We want to do what other people are doing and have what other people have

- We don't want to feel awkward or uncomfortable

- We are afraid of being rejected or made fun of

- We don't know how to get out of a pressure situation

- We aren't sure what we really want.

Dealing with peer pressure

 PowerPoint

1

Be prepared

Think the situation through before it happens. Work out what you would say if someone offered you a cigarette, a drink, asked you to shoplift and so on. If you practise saying your answer out loud at home it will be easier for you to say it when a peer asks you to do something you don't want to do.

2

JUSTINTIME

Avoid the situation

Spend your time with people who don't put you under pressure. Really decent people accept you for who you are. If you have to meet people who make you uncomfortable because they are in your class or in the same club or team, plan to arrive just in time so that there is no chance of having to hang around.

Be proud

Say 'No' and stand up straight and look them in the eye.

Don't apologise, excuse or explain. Do smile if you want to!

Use humour

Say something funny even if it is against yourself! Like: 'I'm too chicken to do anything like that!'

Blame your parents

Most people know what their own parents would think about a particular situation so saying something like, 'You know my mam, she finds out everything!' or 'I can't chance it, I'm already grounded' can get you off the hook.

Be polite

Be polite and mannerly, and smile when you say no (even if that is not how you are feeling on the inside).

People will stop putting pressure on you if they think that you are okay with doing your own thing.

LEARNING LOG

One way in which I have been influenced by peer pressure is _____

_____

_____

One way in which I exert peer pressure on others is _____

_____

_____

Assessment – Check your learning

Peer pressure snap

Divide into groups of two or four. Your teacher assigns one of the cards below to your group. Using the suggestions on pages 92/93, your group has to decide how to deal with the peer pressure situation. Prepare a short role play and perform it for your class or you can perform it and video it for homework.

2 ♥
You have a science exam today. Some of the students tell the teacher that the exam is in two days' time. The teacher asks you when it is.

3 ♥
On the way home from the cinema your three friends share a cigarette. They offer it to you. You have never smoked and do not want to start.

4 ♥
Some classmates want to copy your homework. You do not want to give it to them.

5 ♥
You are staying with your friend. When her parents go out she offers you some vodka. You don't want to take it.

6 ♥
You cycle to school and always wear a helmet. Your friends call you a loser because you won't cycle without it.

7 ♥
You are in a shop on your way home from a school trip and your friends tell you to steal some chocolate.

1 How difficult was it to deal with the situation your group got? Explain your answer.

_____

_____

_____

2 Do you think there is a different way of dealing with peer pressure other than the one your group came up with?

_____

_____

_____

Review of Unit 2: *Substance Use*

1 In this unit I learned about _____

_____

_____

2 I think that this will help me when _____

_____

_____

3 In this unit I liked _____

_____

_____

4 In this unit I did not like _____

_____

_____

5 I would like to find out more about _____

_____

_____

6 This unit links with (name another unit in SPHE or another subject) _____

_____

_____

UNIT 3 Respectful Communication

Learning Outcomes:

This unit helps you to:

1 Understand what communication means ◯

2 Recognise what kind of listener you are ◯

3 Identify the three main types of communication – passive, aggressive, assertive – and understand the differences in each style ◯

(Tick each topic off as you complete it.)

Types of Communication

All our dealings with other people involve communication. This can be:

● Written communication (text, letter, internet)

● Symbols such as road signs

● Gestures such as a thumbs-up

● Speaking to each other.

KEY WORDS

Communication

Body language

Tone

Emphasis

Passive communication

Aggressive communication

Assertive communication

KEY WORDS

Communication

The act or process of using words, sounds, signs, symbols or actions to express or exchange information or ideas, thoughts and feelings, to others.

How we Communicate

While we may think of communication as mainly involving what we say, in fact this accounts for only 7 per cent of the ways in which we communicate.

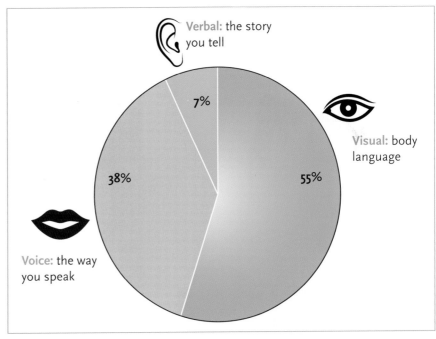

Verbal: the story you tell

7%

Visual: body language

55%

38%

Voice: the way you speak

Body Language

As you can see from the pie chart above the most important part of how we communicate is not what we say (verbal) but how we use our voices (voice) and what body language we use (visual). Body language is also known as **non-verbal communication**.

Did You Know?

Animals, insects and birds can communicate very well using non-verbal communication. From the age of six weeks, a lamb can find its mother in a large flock of sheep by bleating.

Bees use chemical smells (pheromones) to issue alarms and instructions and they do variations of a waggle dance to communicate directions to the rest of the swarm.

Whales communicate through breaching (leaping out of the water), kangaroos thump their hind legs to warn of danger and horses rub noses as a sign of affection. Bottlenose dolphins, who have no vocal cords, communicate through clicks, squawks, whistles and trills, made by the muscles in the hole on the top of their heads.

KEY WORDS

Body language

Sending messages and hints about your feelings, attitudes and moods, through your body posture, movements, gestures, where you stand, your facial expressions and eye movements. The messages communicated by body language can be quite different to your spoken words.

Activity 1

Do you see what I'm saying?

Picture A

Picture B

Examine the two photographs above and answer the following questions:

1 Describe the differences in body language between the two pictures. (Check the explanation of body language in the Key Words box.)

_____

_____

_____

2 What does their body language tell you about the relationship between the two people in each photograph? Be careful to keep your answers to the evidence you can see in the pictures.

_____

_____

_____

Examples of body language

Body language is made up of many different parts. From when we are babies, we understand what our parents' body language means. In school, students can often tell by the way a teacher walks into the classroom what the day's lesson is going to be like!

Activity 2

Types of body language

Look at the chart below which outlines some of the different aspects of body language and see if you can come up with any other examples.

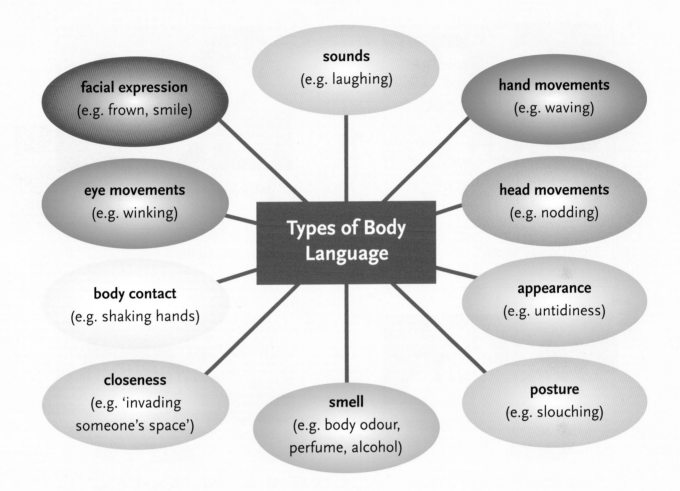

- sounds (e.g. laughing)
- facial expression (e.g. frown, smile)
- hand movements (e.g. waving)
- eye movements (e.g. winking)
- head movements (e.g. nodding)
- body contact (e.g. shaking hands)
- appearance (e.g. untidiness)
- closeness (e.g. 'invading someone's space')
- smell (e.g. body odour, perfume, alcohol)
- posture (e.g. slouching)

Types of Body Language

My examples

_____
_____
_____
_____
_____
_____
_____
_____

Activity 3

Reading body language

Using what you have learned so far, can you identify what message is being given by the body language in the pictures below?

1

① What is the message?

_____

② How do you know?

_____

2

① What is the message?

_____

② How do you know?

_____

3

① What is the message?

_____

② How do you know?

_____

4

① What is the message?

_____

② How do you know?

_____

Tone of voice and emphasis

When people are communicating with each other, even if we do not understand the words or the language we can grasp what is being communicated by both body language and how someone uses their _voice_. Some words have different meanings depending on the _tone_ in which they are said and which words are _stressed_ or _emphasised_. Even a simple word like 'Hey' can have a few different meanings, from 'Hello' to 'What are you doing?' to 'Stop!', depending on how you say it.

Often the way we say something is more important than what we say. If we whisper, shout, pause or speak really fast, it affects the meaning of what we are saying. People also frequently make judgements about other people because of their accents.

Someone's tone of voice can also tell us whether they are enthusiastic or bored, nervous or relaxed. Emphasising or stressing different words in a sentence can also give us clues about the real meaning of what's being said.

KEY WORDS

Tone

The quality of a person's voice: 'He spoke gently.' 'She answered sarcastically.'

Emphasis

To put stress on a syllable, word or phrase to show its importance. This can change the meaning of a sentence.

Did You Know?

Babies understand what their mothers are saying by picking up on the tone of their voice.

Activity 4

It's the way that you say it!

In pairs/groups look at the examples below and practise saying the following sentences, stressing or emphasising the word in **bold** each time you say it.

- **What** do you want?
- What **do** you want?
- What do **you** want?
- What do you **want?**

Now do the same with the following two sentences:

- This has made my day.
- What are you looking at?

1 In your pair/group make up at least two examples where stressing different words in a sentence changes the meaning. Write them down.

_____

_____

2 How did the meaning of the sentences change when different words were emphasised?

_____

_____

3 What did you learn from this activity about how you speak to others?

_____

Did you notice that sometimes the **tone** and **emphasis** of what you say can contradict and completely change the meaning of the words in a sentence? For this reason text messages or comments on social media can backfire, as the reader may not understand that the comment was meant to be a joke.

Listening

Communication is a two-way process. It requires a speaker and a listener.

Listening is important because you can learn new information when you listen carefully to other people. If you pay attention to the person speaking, you can pick up on body language, gestures, expressions and other non-verbal clues that will help you understand what they are really saying.

Listening is a real skill, something that not everyone has but everybody can learn. It is also polite to listen to other people, and it helps you to get along with them. It gives you an insight into a person's thoughts and behaviour which makes dealing with them easier. Sometimes just by listening you can help people see the situation more clearly and to deal better with their emotions.

Sometimes we assume that we know how to listen because it is something we do all of the time – when we listen to music, our friends, teachers and family. Mark in your place on the Listening Line below and then do the activity on page 103 to find out how good a listener you are.

> 'One of the most **sincere** forms of respect is *actually listening* to what **another** has to say.'
>
> Bryant H McGill

Remember the ground rules!

Only share what you are happy with other people knowing.

Activity

5 The Listening Line

1 How well do you listen to others? Mark on the Listening Line below where you would place yourself as a listener.

Poor listener									Good listener
1	2	3	4	5	6	7	8	9	10

2 Talk to two or three others about where you have placed yourself on the line and explain why you chose that position.

Activity 6

Listening quiz

Here are ten statements about listening. Read each sentence and tick whether it is like you or unlike you.

Listening quiz		Like me	Unlike me
1	When the other person is talking I often think about what I am going to say next.		
2	If someone says something I don't agree with I tend to switch off.		
3	I find it hard to look at someone when they are talking to me.		
4	How much I like the person who is speaking affects how I listen to them.		
5	When someone is speaking to me I often interrupt and ask lots of questions.		
6	I rarely notice people's body language (eye contact, expression on their face, hands movements) when they are talking.		
7	When I think I know what someone is going to say I often finish the sentence.		
8	If someone is talking to me I often talk about my experience and say something like 'That reminds me of . . .' or 'That happened to me too and . . .'.		
9	I often answer a question with another question when someone is talking.		
10	Sometimes I stop paying attention to what someone is saying but I pretend to be listening anyway.		
	Total		

Scoring

When you have finished the quiz add up your responses in the 'Like me' boxes and see how good you are as a listener.

Less than 3: You are an excellent listener. Good for you!

4, 5 or 6: You are a good listener, but there is room for improvement!

More than 7: Oh dear! You are not a good listener. You have a lot to learn about listening. But read the next activity and you will pick up tips on how to improve.

Activity 7

How to improve your listening skills

Read the six tips and check out what each one means. In your copybook, rate yourself as 'Like me' or 'Not like me' for each skill. When you have finished, have another look at where you placed yourself on the Listening Line on page 102. Now that you understand more about what it is to be a good listener, see if you would move your position!

2 Don't talk too much! Let the other person speak.

Don't interrupt. Be patient. Use words of encouragement like 'I see', 'Mmm', 'Ah ha'.

1 Be aware of your body language
The way you sit or stand can help the other person feel at ease. Make good eye contact but don't stare. Nod and smile to acknowledge what you have heard. Be relaxed.

3 Listen and look for clues
Prepare yourself to listen by getting rid of distractions. Listen to the words and the tone of voice of the speaker. Listen for the feelings behind the words. Be aware of the person's body language.

4 Learn good questioning skills
Avoid using questions that have a 'Yes' or a 'No' answer (closed questions). Use questions that encourage people to talk, e.g. How? Why do you think? What was that like? But don't ask too many questions.

6 Avoid giving advice
Some people may not want advice, so only give advice if it is asked for. They may just want you to listen to them and this allows them to think their problems through while they are talking.

5 Show you understand
Don't assume you understand. If you are unsure about something ask a question. Use a question like 'Is this what you mean?' Summarise what the person has said every so often, so you will be clear about what you have heard.

 PowerPoint

Activity 8

Six listening types

Your teacher will show you a presentation on the six main types of listener. See if you can work out which one you are . . . and which one you would like to be!

Activity 9

Listening role play

Let's see what you have learned! Join up with another student. Decide which of you will be **A** and who will be **B**. After you have done the role play activity below, answer the questions.

Role play 1

A talks to **B** about his/her favourite film. **B** appears distracted and fidgety and does not listen very well.

Role play 2

B talks to **A** about how s/he spends his/her spare time. **A** listens very well, using the skills he/she has learned.

1. In role play 1 if you are **A**:

   What did **B** do to show that he/she was not listening?

   _____

   _____

   How did you feel when you were speaking and **B** was not listening?

   _____

   _____

2. In role play 2 if you are **B**:

   What did **A** do to show that he/she was listening?

   _____

   _____

   How did you feel when you were speaking and **A** was really listening?

   _____

   _____

As you have taken part in a number of listening activities you should now be able to complete the sentences below:

A good listener is someone who _____

_____

_____

To be a better listener I need to _____

_____

_____

LEARNING LOG

Communication Styles

When we communicate with other people we usually use one of three main communication styles:

1 **Passive communication**

2 **Aggressive communication**

3 **Assertive communication**

A communication style is the way in which information is conveyed to others. Again, in communication style, we all use non-verbal cues that are more important than the words we say. These clues include eye contact, facial expressions, gestures, tone of voice, touch and how close we stand to someone (personal space).

By knowing the different communication styles, and understanding their effect on your dealings with others, you can become more effective communicators. You will be able to recognise these styles in others and know how to deal with them in a respectful way.

COMMUNICATION STYLES

	Passive	Agressive	Assertive
Verbal Cues	• Afraid to speak up • Voice is meek and apologetic	• Interrupts and talks over you • Voice is loud, maybe shouts	• Speaks openly and says what they mean • Uses ordinary, non-threatening tone
Body Language	• Avoids looking directly at you • Poor eye contact • Little or no expression • Slouches, withdraws	• Stares or eyeballs you • Intimidating • Rigid, arms on hips • May invade your personal space	• Open, relaxed stance • Shows expressions which match what they are saying • Good eye contact
Their Style	• Isolates themselves from the group • Powerless • Values self less than others • Resentful • Dismissed • Agrees with others in spite of their own opinion	• Sarcastic • Impatient • Rude • Controls the group • Values self more than others • Only considers their own feelings or opinions	• Respectful • Sensitive to others • Confident • Participates in the group • Keeps to the point • Able to see other people's point of view • Values self equally with others
Result	• Does not reach goals and may not know them • Gives into what you want	• Gets what they want and walks over others on the way	• Usually reaches goals, or a good compromise which is acceptable to others
	I'm not OK – you're OK	I'm OK – you're not OK	I'm OK – you're OK

Activity 10 Recognising the different communication styles

Using examples from TV, books and films, complete the table below with the name of a character, who behaves and communicates passively, aggressively and assertively.

	Name of character	Description of behaviour
Passive communicator		
Aggressive communicator		
Assertive communicator		

Activity 11 The sleepover

Your teacher will show you a clip of three styles of communication. When you have seen all three use the information in the **Communication Styles table** to identify which scene (A, B or C) is:

Assertive: _____ Evidence: _____

Passive: _____ Evidence: _____

Aggressive: _____ Evidence: _____

❶ Which communication style led to the best outcome?
_____

❷ Why? _____

▶ Animation

LEARNING LOG

Write a poem, song or rap about any aspect of communication, using what you have learned in this topic.

Useful Websites

www.reachout.com – go to communication styles and learn some helpful information

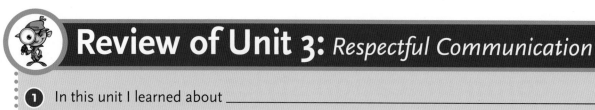

Review of Unit 3: *Respectful Communication*

1 In this unit I learned about _____

_____

_____

2 I think that this will help me when _____

_____

_____

3 In this unit I liked _____

_____

_____

4 In this unit I did not like _____

_____

_____

5 I would like to find out more about _____

_____

_____

6 This unit links with (name another unit in SPHE or another subject) _____

_____

_____

Minding Myself and Others

Learning Outcomes:

This unit helps you to:

1. Be clear about what bullying means
2. Talk about different types of bullying
3. Know about the role of bystanders in bullying
4. Identify how to deal with incidents of bullying
5. Examine your school's policies on bullying and internet safety and be aware of what they mean for your behaviour and safety.

(Tick each topic off as you complete it.)

KEY WORDS

Bullying

Repeated, unwanted, aggressive behaviour, verbal, emotional or physical, directed by an individual or group against others. Bullying can happen when people are any age, are in any place – like school, university, work – and it can be carried on for a long or a short time.

KEY WORDS

Bullying

Cyberbullying

Relational bullying

Bystanders

Understanding and Recognising Bullying

It is important that you feel safe and happy in school. Sometimes things can happen which can make you feel that your school is not such a safe place. Bullying is one example of this.

Activity 1

Bullying – how much do you know?

We have all heard of bullying and most people think they know what it means. Read each of the statements below and find out how much you really know about bullying. Decide if you Agree, Disagree or are Unsure and tick the relevant box. Then answer the questions below. Your teacher will go through the correct answers later.

	Statements	Agree	Disagree	Unsure
1	Bullying is just a bit of fun.			
2	There is no bullying in this school.			
3	Bullying can be just a one-off incident.			
4	Some people take bullying too seriously.			
5	Bullying is deliberately carried out to hurt someone.			
6	There is more bullying among boys than girls.			
7	Girls and boys use different ways to bully people.			
8	Everyone is bullied sometimes.			
9	If a person is bullied they should tell someone.			
10	Everyone has a responsibility to stop bullying.			
11	I know what to do in my school if I am being bullied.			
12	There are different kinds of bullying.			
13	If I am being bullied, I will always know who is doing it.			

📧 PowerPoint

1 Which statement had you the most difficulty in choosing a response to?

_____

_____

_____

2 Which statement surprised you the most?

_____

_____

_____

Types of Bullying

Physical: Fighting, hitting, spitting, pinching, poking, tripping, pushing

Cyberbullying: Using information technology, like mobiles, laptops or tablets, to post hurtful information about someone online or to send nasty emails, texts or messages on social media websites like Snapchat or Facebook, or to upload embarrassing or damaging photos of them

Extortion: Demanding money by threats or forcing someone to hand over their property

Intimidation: Making people feel frightened, scared or uncomfortable by using threatening gestures, aggressive body language, tone of voice, facial expressions or ganging up on a person

Name calling: Shouting hurtful, humiliating insults and comments about someone, especially about their body size, the colour of their hair, their clothes, family, accent and academic ability – good or bad

Relational bullying: Isolating, excluding, ignoring, spreading rumours, passing notes, whispering, rolling eyes, mimicking, smirking behind someone's back

Damaging property: Breaking, stealing or hiding someone else's property or defacing it including their clothes, schoolbag, homework, pencil case, books, mobile phone or their lunch

Identity-based: Name calling or violence against those who are disabled, gay, perceived to be gay, a different race, colour or ethnic background, a member of the travelling community or who have special educational needs

Did You Know?

Even though bullying is normally behaviour that is repeated for a long time, posting a one-off offensive or hurtful public message or image on a social network site or other public medium, e.g. mobiles, where it can be viewed, copied or forwarded by other people, is still regarded as bullying.

Assessment – Check your learning

On your own or in a small group, decide whether each of the ten scenarios below is bullying. Write 'Yes' or 'No' in the middle column. If you answer 'Yes' write the type of bullying in the last column. You might need to write two or three types of bullying into the last column for some of the answers. Your teacher will go through the answers later.

	Statements	Yes or no	Type of bullying
1	Mary continuously makes snide remarks about Gina's new hair style. Others have started to join in. Gina is embarrassed and upset and Mary knows this.		
2	Peter doesn't like Mike. He meets him in the corridor and deliberately knocks Mike's lunch out of his hand.		
3	Pat, a second year student, tells Jack, who is in first year, that he will 'get him' on the way home if he doesn't hand over his lunch money. Jack has handed over money in the past so Pat knows that Jack is an easy target.		
4	Joanne bumps into Maura in the corridor and knocks her down. She helps her up and asks if she is okay.		
5	Cora sends cruel, anonymous text messages to Jean. Cora says Jean has BO. Other girls know about the texts and it usually happens when Cora is with a group of friends. Jean sees them sniggering when she is checking her text messages.		
6	Gerry doesn't like Ali. Ali is quite self-confident and this doesn't bother him. Gerry has started to call him names and say Ali is 'gay'. He has also written nasty comments about Ali in notes to other students.		
7	Patricia and Asha don't want to be friends with Janet. When she walks past, they hold their noses as though she smells.		
8	Tom is a bit of a loner in school and his classmates make fun of him. Paul hides Tom's schoolbag, so Tom gets into trouble in class for not having his homework.		
9	Rose invited Orla to babysit with her, but Orla's mother won't allow her to go. Now Rose posts hurtful comments on Orla's Facebook page.		
10	Bilal loves science and continuously gets praise from his teacher for his good work. Now some boys in his class have started to 'hiss' quietly when this happens. This does not bother Bilal at all and he continues to work hard.		

Effects of Bullying

As well as affecting your self-esteem, bullying can cause physical injury, stress and make you feel very isolated and alone. If you are being bullied, you can feel like there's nothing you can do about it without making it worse, which is pretty scary.

Activity

2

Being bullied

This activity can be done on your own, in pairs or in small groups.

1. Around the outside of the body write all the effects of bullying that you would be able to see (physical).

2. On the inside of the body write all of the effects of bullying that are not visible (emotional, social), for example, finding it hard to sleep.

3. In a different-coloured pen write in what you think the effects of physical, social and emotional bullying might be on the bully.

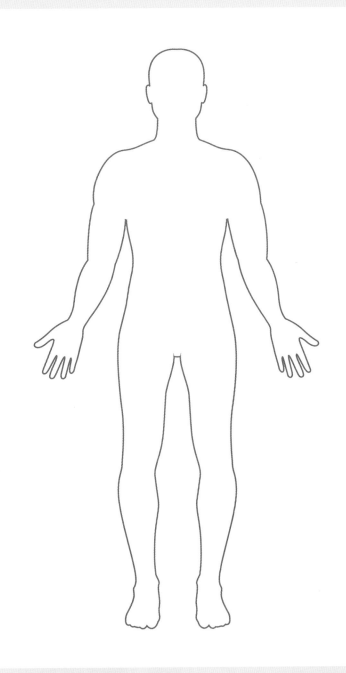

4 When everyone is finished look at the body shapes of your classmates/the other groups. If they have anything different, add it to your own list.

5 Which effects of bullying do you think are the most serious?

_____

_____

6 Which effects last longer than others?

_____

_____

7 Apart from the bully and the victim, make a list of people who can be affected by bullying.

_____

_____

Many children who are being bullied are afraid to speak out. They are scared something worse will happen if they tell someone about the bullying. Reports have shown that as young people grow older, they are less likely to tell someone they are being bullied. They become more and more isolated and can experience depression and other health problems.

Bystanders and bullying

Bystanders can play a very important role in bullying. Below are some actions they might take:

Negative action

- Join in on the bullying themselves
- Stand on the sideline, making comments and laughing (bullies love an audience)
- Walk away and ignore it
- Look on silently even though they see it happening.

Positive action

- Join up with other bystanders to help the victim
- Report the bullying to an adult
- Support the victim
- Try to stop the bullying by talking to the bully and the victim (50 per cent of bullying stops if bystanders intervene).

KEY WORDS

Bystanders

People who see someone being bullied or know bullying is going on. Stopping bullying is not just the responsibility of the person being bullied. Often the bully's victim feels too powerless or scared to do anything or to tell anyone that they are being bullied. Bystanders have a responsibility to do something about it.

Did You Know?

As a bystander if you are not part of the solution, you are part of the problem!

Activity 3

What type of bystander are you?

Using one of the slogans below make a poster or write a poem on the role of bystanders in bullying:

- If you are not part of the solution you are part of the problem!

- Don't just stand there – do something!

- Bullying! See it, Get Help, Stop it!

- If you knew about it – you're part of it.

Dealing with Bullying

There are things you can do to deal with bullying if you see it happening or if you are being bullied. The most important and effective one is to tell someone you trust about it.

If the bullying is happening in your school, you should check out the school's Anti-Bullying Policy. This is usually on the school's website. It will tell you what to do.

If you are being bullied, you could:

- **Avoid the situation** – if the bullying is happening in the queue for the school shop, bring your lunch and don't use the shop. If it happens between classes get organised so that you leave class with the majority of the students and are not on your own. Don't be the last in the changing rooms, at the lockers or in the toilets.

- **Use humour** – if it is safe to do so. For example, if the bully says 'You're ugly' you could reply: 'We can't all be as good looking as you!'

- **Be assertive** – if a bully asks you for your homework look them straight in the eye and say 'No, you need to do your own homework!', or just say a plain 'No'. If someone says 'You're stupid' say 'That's not true' or 'I know I'm not and that's all that matters!'

- **Positive self-talk** – tell yourself that you are a good, worthwhile person. Remind yourself that you are loved. Sometimes it helps to remind yourself that you will be home in a few hours and away from this bully.

- **Ignore it** – bullies get a thrill from seeing the upset and hurt they cause. If you don't let them see that you are upset, by ignoring them and not responding, they often give up.

- **Walk away** – this is linked to ignoring bullies. If you are able to walk away, do so. This is easier if you have a group you can hang around with or if you can stay with the main group of your class.

- **Approach the person involved if it is safe to do so** – you have to be quite brave to do this, but if you think it might work, make sure the bully is on their own and in a reasonably public place. Tell them what they are doing to you is wrong and that you want it to stop. Don't get into an argument with them. Just say your piece and walk away.

- **Make new friends** – sometimes you may have to leave a group if they start bullying you. You can make new friends with other people in your class, by taking up a sport or new activity, joining a club or learning to play a musical instrument.

🖥 **PowerPoint**

Remember!

There are different ways of dealing with bullying and some approaches suit some situations better than others. For example, if you can never see yourself making a funny remark to the bully, then ignoring them or walking away might be better tactics for you to try. What is important is that you take some action – whether it's telling someone about the bullying, avoiding the situation or making new friends. Work on what suits you.

Cyberbullying

Parents Warned on Cyberbullying

Irish Daily Report
9 March 2017

Bullying is no longer a problem that only occurs in the playgrounds, hallways and lunch rooms of schools across the country. Instead, new technology such as mobile phones, smartphones, tablets and laptops, are contributing to an alarming change in the different ways children are being bullied. Cyberbullying is the only form of bullying where a single incident can be seen as bullying. This is because a single post can be copied or forwarded and seen by thousands and the potential for someone being hurt is much greater. Cyberbullying also brings bullying into the victim's home, often the victim's bedroom, which means they have no safe place or time to get away from the bully. It is also nastier as the bully does not have to be in direct contact with the victim and can be anonymous. Cyberbullying is often group bullying and can make the victim feel totally isolated and helpless as they don't know how to stop it.

Activity
4

Cyberbullying: test your knowledge!

Check your knowledge of cyberbullying by taking the quiz below. Tick True or False to answer each question. Your teacher will go through the answers later.

	Cyberbullying	True	False
1	Cyberbullying means using technology to harass or intimidate someone.		
2	Cyberbullying can happen using: ● Mobile phones ● Facebook ● All of these. ● Instant messages ● Instagram ● Email ● Snapchat		
3	Most victims of cyberbullying tell someone about it.		
4	You can say anything you want online as no one can find out who you are.		
5	If your friends cyberbully then you are more likely to do it too.		
6	People cyberbully because: ● They are jealous ● They think it's a joke ● They are insecure ● They want revenge ● All of these.		
7	People who are traditional bullies are more likely to be cyberbullies.		
8	Most young people experience cyberbullying.		
9	The best way to prove you have been a victim of cyberbullying is to: ● Reply to the bully ● Delete the message, image or email ● Tell your friend that you were bullied ● Save the texts, emails or screenshots of the unpleasant message ● Tell an adult.		
10	Responding to a bully by sending a mean message can make the situation go from bad to worse. It could even be dangerous.		

Did You Know?

Flaming
Flaming is when you say mean things, usually in ALL CAPS, and often in a public forum, with the intention of humiliating someone.

IP address
Every device linked to the Internet has a unique number assigned to it, called an IP address. All messages can be traced back to the device (smartphone, laptop, tablet and so on) from which they were sent by using the IP address.

You Loser

Cyberbullying can take the form of:

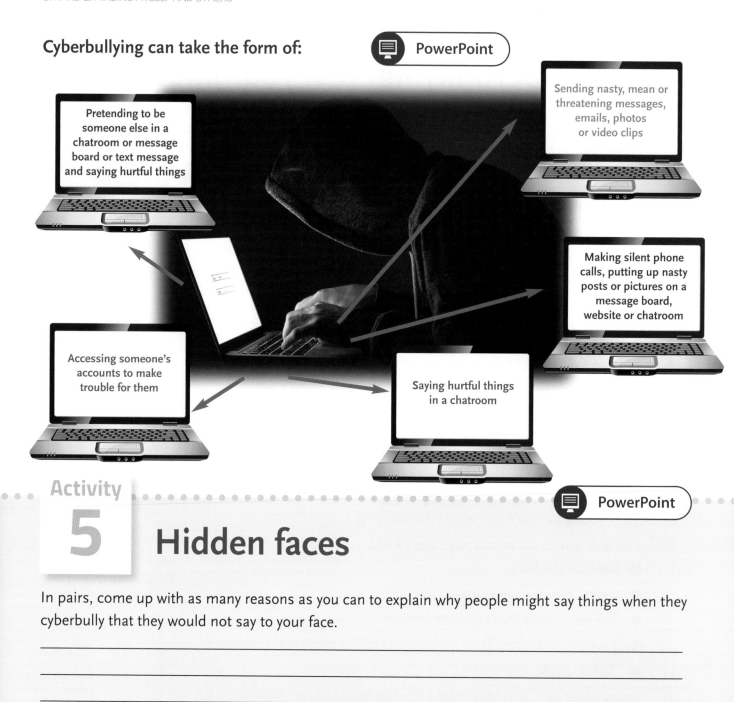

Pretending to be someone else in a chatroom or message board or text message and saying hurtful things

Sending nasty, mean or threatening messages, emails, photos or video clips

Making silent phone calls, putting up nasty posts or pictures on a message board, website or chatroom

Accessing someone's accounts to make trouble for them

Saying hurtful things in a chatroom

PowerPoint

Activity 5

Hidden faces

PowerPoint

In pairs, come up with as many reasons as you can to explain why people might say things when they cyberbully that they would not say to your face.

_____

_____

_____

_____

_____

Activity 6

Cyberbullying case studies

Read about Mark and Kim below and, using what you have already learned about cyberbullying, answer the questions.

Mark is in first year and spends loads of time studying. His parents want him to do well but his test results aren't very good. He gets a lot of slagging over this. He often gets posts and text messages during the day and at night calling him a 'LOSER' and they're getting worse every day.

This morning he got a text from a number he did not recognise, with a photo of his body with a clown's head on it. There was a thought bubble above the picture with the words: 'Why am I so STUPID? What kind of a clown am I?' Mark thinks Chloe, the most popular girl in the first year, is behind the message.

1 What forms of cyberbullying do the students use on Mark? What is your evidence?

_____

_____

2 How do you think Mark feels? What parts of the cyberbullying make him feel this way?

_____

_____

3 Do you think Mark should tell his parents about the cyberbullying?

_____

_____

4 Do you think Mark should tell his school about the cyberbullying?

_____

_____

Kim is pretty popular. She is running for First Year Representative on the Student Council. The election is a week away and Kim seems to have the same amount of support as Maeve. Maeve's friends decide to sabotage Kim. They create a fake Facebook page for her, using a bad photo for her profile picture, and for her interests, they write: partying, making fun of anything ASIAN, loving myself.

Many of the students at the school are Asian and rumours start to spread that Kim is a racist. During the two days before the election, Maeve's friends start to flame Kim almost every hour, with texts that say things like 'RACIST'.

1 What forms of cyberbullying do Maeve's friends use on Kim? What is your evidence?

_____

_____

2 Do you think there is ever a good reason for impersonating someone else online or creating a profile about them?

_____

_____

3 Do you think Maeve knows what her friends are doing? What is Maeve's responsibility in this?

_____

_____

4 What do you think the consequences should be for Maeve and her friends if the school finds out?

_____

Your school's policy on cyberbullying

Now that you know about cyberbullying and what it involves, answer the questions below about your school's policy on dealing with this problem.

1 What does your school's Anti-Bullying Policy say about cyberbullying?

_____

_____

_____

2 Is there any other school policy which deals with cyberbullying?

_____

_____

_____

Don't forget that nothing is permanently deleted. Even sites like Snapchat which claim to remove files can't guarantee this. Anyone can make a screen-grab of a Snapchat.

Assessment – Check your learning

Bullying Scenarios

Your teacher will assign one of the following three problems for you to work on. Write your answers below.

1 *Peter's problem*

Read about Peter's problem and then answer the questions below.

Peter has tried to make friends with others in his class ever since he came into first year at Christmas. He has just moved into the area and none of his friends are in this school. Two boys in particular, John and Mark, deliberately ignore him and laugh at him behind his back. In a soccer competition between the first-year classes Peter did not play well and now John is blaming him for their team losing. He has started spreading rumours and calling Peter names. John has also taken Peter's schoolbag and hidden it on a number of occasions. This is making Peter's life miserable. He is finding it difficult to concentrate on his work and is getting into trouble because he is often late for class as he tries to avoid John. Peter doesn't know what to do. He is afraid to tell anyone because John picks his time to bully Peter when there is no one else looking.

1 What are the ways in which John is bullying Peter?

_____

_____

_____

2 Describe how Peter feels, using as many feeling words as you can think of:

_____

_____

3 What advice would you give to Peter?

_____

_____

4 Who else could have helped and how?

_____

_____

2 The rumour mill

Read about Maria's situation and then answer the questions below.

Maria missed a birthday party and sleepover in Ava's house last month. Most of her friends were there, but Maria had to babysit that night. Since then Ava and some of the other girls have been telling lies about Maria and spreading rumours about her. At lunchtime they refuse to let her sit with them. Maria sees Ava and the others looking at her and giggling and laughing. They also get out ahead of her when school finishes and Maria has to walk home on her own. Maria knows that Liz is having a party next Saturday and that Ava has told Liz not to invite Maria.

1 What are the ways in which Ava is bullying Maria?

_____

_____

_____

2 Describe how Maria feels, using as many feeling words as you can think of:

_____

_____

3 What advice would you give to Maria?

_____

_____

4 Who else could have helped and how?

_____

_____

③ Picking on Paul

Read about Paul's predicament and then answer the questions below.

Paul seems to get into trouble a lot, for all sorts of reasons, including being late for class, not having work done and forgetting his PE gear. He gets upset when this happens. Paul wants to fit into the class but no one wants to be friends with him because of the way he behaves. Marian and Michael and others in the class know that it is easy to upset Paul and they often do things to annoy him, like hiding his coat or his lunch and tripping him up and pushing him deliberately.

Last week somebody wrote hurtful things about him on a desk and on a toilet door. When Paul discovered this he got very upset and angry and started to kick his locker. Again, he was the one who was caught and once again got into trouble.

① What are the ways in which Paul is being bullied?

_____

_____

_____

② Describe how Paul feels, using as many feeling words as you can think of:

_____

_____

③ What advice would you give to Paul?

_____

_____

_____

④ Who else could have helped and how?

_____

_____

_____

_____

If I saw someone being bullied
two things I would do are:
1
2

LEARNING LOG

Useful Websites

www.barnardos.ie – for helpful tips and advice on cyberbullying

www.childline.ie – to find out about internet safety

Activity 8

Making your school a safer place

If you were being bullied what could you do? Look at your school's Anti-Bullying Policy and write down two things that you could do to make your school become a safer place for you and other students. Then, in groups of four and using the Anti-Bullying Policy, research the answers to questions 3–6 below.

1 _____

_____

2 _____

_____

3 Who should you tell in your school if you are being bullied?

_____

4 Can you report bullying anonymously?

_____

5 What are the sanctions for bullying in this school?

_____

_____

6 Am I allowed to have my mobile phone in school?

_____

STRAND 2: MINDING MYSELF AND OTHERS

Review of Unit 4: *Anti-Bullying*

1 In this unit I learned about _____
_____
_____

2 I think that this will help me when _____
_____
_____

3 In this unit I liked _____
_____
_____

4 In this unit I did not like _____
_____
_____

5 I would like to find out more about _____
_____
_____

6 This unit links with (name another unit in SPHE or another subject) _____
_____
_____

UNIT 1 Having a Friend and Being a Friend

Learning Outcomes:

This unit helps you to:

1. Appreciate the value of friendships ○
2. Explore how your friendships may change over time ○
3. Identify the qualities that you value in a friend ○
4. Think about how you are as a friend. ○

(Tick each topic off as you complete it.)

KEY WORDS

Friend
Friendship
Acquaintances
Relationships

Friendships

Now that you are a teenager, your friendships and relationships are usually more important to you than when you were younger. As you become more independent you spend less time with your parents and family. Through your friendships you learn how to socialise and get on with other people. You learn how to be sensitive to the thoughts and feelings of others, and how to give and take support when you or your friends find life tough.

Some of you have many friends while other students in your class have just one or two friends. It is different for everyone. Some of you have a best friend while others don't.

Not all friends are best friends or even close friends. Your friends can range from close to not so close. Some of your friends may be *casual friends* or *acquaintances*, who you share an interest with or who you might work with on a school project. Other friends may be *close friends*. You hang around with them outside school or go to the cinema with them. These friends are closer to you than your casual friends.

Then you may have one or two *best friends*. They know all about you and you know all about them. You can share your feelings and worries with them without fear of being judged. They support you in times of difficulty and you are there for them too.

You may also have different types of friend. Some of your friends are fun to be with, while you like others because they are kind and good listeners.

The friend you have can change throughout your life for many different reasons. For example, you or they might move house or school, or you might get involved in different things.

As you go through life you will make new friends and you might lose contact with earlier ones. Maybe you may not see some of the friends you had in primary school any more (equally you may still be close to some of them). You may start to make new friends through your involvement in sports, new hobbies, Irish college, clubs or even within your family and neighbourhood.

Activity

1 Friendship circles

Think about your friendships now and write the names of all your friends in the 'Circles of friendship' diagram on page 127. If you'd prefer not to write names, then you could use a symbol or drawing instead.

- Write your own name in the centre
- In the next circle write the name(s) of your good friend(s)
- In the outside circle write the names of your casual friends, those you know well enough to talk to but not as well as your good friends
- In the outer circle write the names of acquaintances.

When you've completed your 'Circles of friendship' discuss it with one or two others and then answer the questions.

1 What did you learn about your friendships?

_____

_____

2 How did you decide what friends should go in each circle?

_____

_____

Casual friends

Close friends

Good friend

3 Why might there be differences between your friendship circles and those of others in your group?

_____

_____

4 If you would like to bring a friend from the outer circles closer to you, how might you do this?

_____

_____

5 Write three things that you can do to nurture your closest friendships.

_____

_____

Qualities of a True Friend

Activity 2

A true friend

Think about your friends, the ones you have now or friends you had in the past, and write down the three qualities that you value most in them. What do/did you like about them? You can look at the list below to help you. Then join with another student and combine your lists. You now have six qualities.

1 Discuss why each of these qualities is important to you.

2 Then rank them in order, according to how much you value each quality with 1 being the most important quality, 2 being next important and so on.

3 Take a class vote on what you think are the most important qualities of a true friend and represent these on a bar chart like the one below.

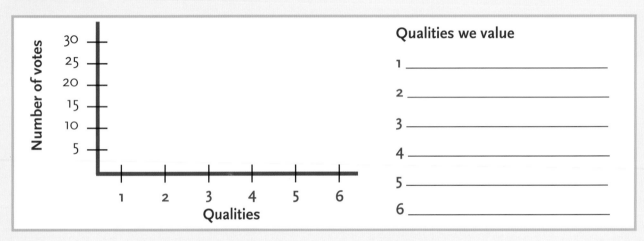

Qualities we value

1 _____
2 _____
3 _____
4 _____
5 _____
6 _____

What is a true friend?

a A true friend lets you have other friends.

b A true friend understands and accepts how much your parents allow you to do.

c A true friend is someone you can tell something private to.

d A true friend allows you to do things your own way.

e A true friend makes you feel good about yourself.

f A true friend is not jealous of your success.

g A true friend doesn't talk about you behind your back.

h A true friend shares with you and is not mean.

i A true friend doesn't force you to do something you don't want to do.

j A true friend is interested in what is good for you.

k A true friend tells you when you are wrong.

> The *only way* to have *a friend* is to be one.
>
> (Ralph Waldo Emerson)

Activity 3

Ask the agony aunt

 Animation

As you go through life you will have plenty of chances to make new friends but sometimes making a new friend can be difficult, especially as you move from primary to post-primary school. The emails to the agony aunt Amy below are from two students starting out in first year.

With another student, discuss the emails and decide what advice you would give to Jane and Olaf if you were Amy. Write your reply below.

Listen to the advice that others have suggested and see if you agree or disagree with it.

To:	Amy
From:	Jane

Dear Amy,

I am starting secondary school soon and I'm worried about making friends. I am a bit quiet and a little shy. My best friend and my other friends from primary school are all going to other schools. The girls from my primary school who are coming to my new school are in a different class, except for two girls who were friendlier with each other than with me in my old school. I'm really worried about break and lunch time as I stay in school for lunch and don't want to be on my own. What should I do?

Thanks,

Jane

To:	Jane
From:	Amy

Hi Jane,

_____

_____

_____

_____

_____

_____

_____

_____

Amy

To:	Amy
From:	Olaf

Dear Amy

Since I started first year I am really busy. We have loads of homework and three evenings a week I have to stay back for sports training as I hope to make the team next month. I never get time to meet my friends anymore. I'm afraid they'll stop bothering about me and begin to leave me out. Already they go to after-school study together and I can't because of training.

Is there anything I can do? Please help!

Olaf

To:	Olaf
From:	Amy

Hi Olaf,

_____

_____

_____

_____

_____

_____

_____

Amy

Three things which I now value in a friendship are:

1 _____

_____

2 _____

_____

3 _____

_____

LEARNING LOG

Making and Keeping Friends

After listening to the advice given to Jane and Olaf you should have some ideas about how you can make and keep friends. Here are some more tips.

Make an effort to remember everyone's name.

Be interested in others. Don't talk about yourself all the time.

Make a start. Be friendly. Smile and make eye contact. Don't wait for someone else to make the first move. Show you are interested.

TOP TIPS FOR MAKING FRIENDS AND KEEPING THEM!

If there's a problem in your friendship be prepared to talk about it. This shows that you value your friend, you want to be open about how you feel and understand how they feel about the situation.

Join a club or take up a new hobby. Get involved!

Be honest about yourself. Don't try to be somebody you are not.

Be kind and generous, in word and deed.

Don't boast or brag! Most people don't like show-offs.

Don't be afraid to share what is important to you – your opinions and your feelings.

Don't be cruel, gossip or spread rumours.

Be a good listener. (Remember you learned about this in previous SPHE classes!)

Accept others as they are, not as who you would like them to be. Your friends won't all be exactly like you and that's what makes friendships different and interesting.

LEARNING LOG

Read through the tips again and identify one quality that you feel is true of you now and one quality that you would like to work on.

One quality that is true of me now is _____

One quality that I would like to work on is _____

Activity 4

The family holiday

Your family is going abroad on holiday and you can bring one friend with you. You have a difficult choice to make!

Here are your friends. Who will you ask to come with you?

Helen/Harry

You have got friendly with Helen/Harry this year. S/He is really popular in your class and if you invited her/him your popularity might increase. Helen/Harry's family is really well-off and last year you went away with them for a long weekend.

Melissa/Mark

You have become quite friendly with Melissa/Mark in the last year. You knew her/him slightly from Saturday morning football, before you started post-primary school. S/He loves sport, music and dancing. You know you would have great fun if Melissa/Mark came along.

Kiya/Kieran

Kiya/Kieran is a bit quiet and does not have many friends. S/He studies a lot and always does really well in exams. S/He has helped you a good few times with your homework. You feel that you should ask Kiya/Kieran along to repay her/him but you are afraid your holiday would not be very exciting if s/he came.

Nina/Nelson

You have known Nina/Nelson for years. S/He was your best friend in primary school and you still do lots of things together. S/He is loyal and a great listener. Nina/Nelson helped you through a tough time in first year when you had problems at home. You know you can depend on her/him.

1 Who did you decide to ask?

_____

2 Why did you choose that person?

_____

 Animation

3 How do you think the friends you did not invite might feel?

_____

_____

4 How would you explain your choice to the friends you did not ask along? Do you have to explain to them?

_____

_____

_____

REMEMBER

Your choice will be guided by what you **value** in your friendships. Your values are what you consider to be important. They usually guide your decisions and choices. In the scenarios above these values might be fun, loyalty, popularity, money and respect. As you grow up, your values may change, and with those changes your friendships may change also. Sometimes, as in this situation, you may have to make a choice between competing values. This can be difficult.

5 Think about the person you chose to take on holidays with you. What values guided your choice?

The values that guided my choice were _____

_____

_____

Three things that I value in my friends now that I might not have valued when I was younger are:

1 _____

2 _____

3 _____

LEARNING LOG

Assessment – Check your learning

Available, One Friend

Using the insights you have gained into friendship and how you think you are as a friend, finish the poster below. The poster should be about you and it should be true. You should list your good qualities as a friend in a colourful and fun way. You may use words, symbols, drawings, pictures or photographs to do this.

Available, One Friend

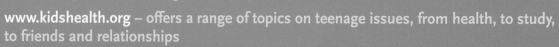

Useful Websites

http://girlshealth.gov – offers girls reliable, useful information on health, relationships and wellbeing

www.kidshealth.org – offers a range of topics on teenage issues, from health, to study, to friends and relationships

Review of Unit 1: *Having a Friend and Being a Friend*

1. In this unit I learned about _____

_____

_____

2. I think that this will help me when _____

_____

_____

3. In this unit I liked _____

_____

_____

4. In this unit I did not like _____

_____

_____

5. I would like to find out more about _____

_____

_____

6. This unit links with (name another unit in SPHE or another subject) _____

_____

_____

UNIT 2 Sexuality, Gender Identity and Sexual Health: Changes at Adolescence – What's Happening Inside Your Body?

Learning Outcomes:

This unit helps you to:

1. Recognise the physical changes that take place in boys and girls during puberty ○

2. Learn about the parts of the male and female reproductive systems and explain what they do ○

3. Understand how pregnancy begins. You will learn more about the development of the baby in the mother's womb in SPHE years 2 and 3. ○

(Tick each topic off as you complete it.)

Changes During Puberty

In earlier SPHE classes you learned about the changes that take place in your body during puberty – the physical, emotional, psychological and social changes. For example, you have learned that the pituitary gland in the brain produces hormones which travel in the blood to the sexual glands to activate them. These sexual glands are the testes in a boy and the ovaries in a girl. The testes produce testosterone and the ovaries produce oestrogen and progesterone. Now we will take a look at all these changes in a bit more detail.

KEY WORDS

Puberty

Ovaries

Testes

Menstruation

Sexual intercourse

Ovulation

Ejaculation

Wet dream

Pregnancy

KEY WORDS

Puberty

The time when your body physically changes from a child's body to the body of a young man or woman. These changes happen gradually, over a number of years.

Did You Know?

Puberty, for girls can happen any time between ages nine to fourteen and for boys, slightly later, any time between ages ten to fifteen. Everybody is different but if you are worried about what is happening to you, do talk to a parent/guardian or another adult that you trust.

Activity

1 Becoming an adult

Read Anne's story and then Barry's story and, with two other students, answer the questions. Ask your teacher for help if you are unsure of the answers.

Anne and Barry are about to begin their journey towards adulthood.

Some of the changes that Barry will experience

His body shape will change. Barry's arms and legs will get longer and muscles will develop on his shoulders, chest and legs. Hair will grow on his face, chest, under arms, around his penis (known as pubic hair) and maybe on his legs. Hormone activity will make his voice 'break' and become deeper. His skin may become oily, resulting in blocked pores and he may have acne on his face, neck and back. He will perspire more, which may result in body odour and he might need to wash more often.

Barry's penis will grow longer and thicker. His testes will be held in a sac-like pouch of wrinkly tissue called the scrotum. Barry's testes will grow larger and begin to produce sperm. A narrow tube, called a sperm duct, carries sperm from the testes to the urethra. Barry may have erections, as his penis becomes filled with blood and becomes hard. This might happen when he is asleep or spontaneously, at any time. If it happens in his sleep he may have a 'wet dream'. This happens when the penis becomes erect and some semen, the liquid which contains the sperm, comes out. Barry may find that his PJs are sticky and wet when he wakes up. This is perfectly normal and nothing to worry about.

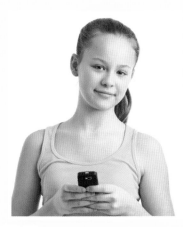

Some of the changes that Anne will experience

Anne's body shape will also be changing. She may gain weight and her hips might widen. Her figure becomes curvier. Gradually her breasts will begin to develop. Hair will grow under her arms and between her legs (known as pubic hair). Her skin may become oilier, resulting in blocked pores which may lead to spots or acne on her face, neck and shoulders. She may perspire more and she will become aware that good hygiene, including regular washing, will prevent body odour developing.

Perhaps the most noticeable change for Anne will be the start of menstruation (having her periods), where the uterus (womb) sheds its lining of tissue and blood. Her periods may be irregular for the first few months, but they will soon settle down to a cycle (menstrual cycle) of around 28 days. She will learn to use sanitary towels or tampons to cope with this (see page 140).

Between her periods Anne will notice a sticky mucous discharge on her underwear. This is perfectly normal and indicates that Anne's body is maturing to prepare her for the time, in the future, when she might become pregnant.

1   What three questions might Anne have about puberty? How would you answer these?

_____

_____

_____

_____

2   What three questions might Barry have about puberty? How would you answer these?

_____

_____

_____

_____

3   Who might Anne or Barry go to if they had any concerns about their bodies during puberty?

_____

_____

_____

_____

LEARNING LOG

Identify two things that you can do to help you cope and feel good about yourself at this time.

_____

_____

_____

Through Adolescence to Becoming a Parent

Introduction

The changes that are taking place in your body during puberty are preparing your body so that one day you can become a father or a mother. Just because your body is physically ready to become a parent doesn't mean that you are. There are a lot of other changes taking place as well.

You are changing in the ways that you think and feel, and in the way you relate to other people, especially to your family. This process of change takes several years until you become an adult. Then you will be ready to become a parent.

Conception

When you are in a long-term, loving relationship, where you are committed to another person you may want to show that love in a special way by making love or having sex. This is often described as 'sleeping together' (you are not really asleep!). When a man and a woman have sex a baby may be conceived (made). **(Conception)**

Sexual intercourse

When a man and a woman are very close and cuddle together two things can happen. The man's penis becomes stiff and erect (having an erection). The woman's vagina becomes wet and slippery. If they decide to make love, it is now possible for the man to put his penis into the woman's vagina (sexual intercourse). This is a pleasurable experience for both the man and the woman. Sperm are released (between 50 and 150 million of them!) from the penis (ejaculation) into the vagina. They swim up through the womb (uterus) and into the fallopian tubes.

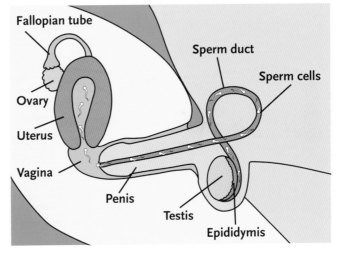

Ovulation

Every month an egg (ovum) is released from one of the ovaries (ovulation), see Diagram 1, and it travels along the fallopian tube waiting for a sperm to fertilise it.

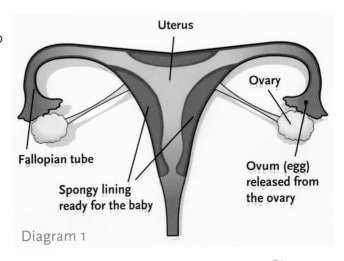

Diagram 1

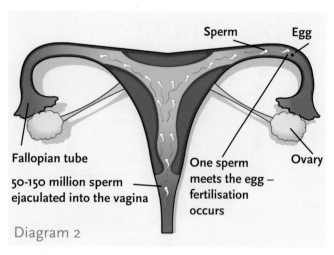

Sperm   Egg

Fallopian tube

50-150 million sperm ejaculated into the vagina

One sperm meets the egg – fertilisation occurs

Ovary

Diagram 2

Fertilisation

If the egg (ovum) meets a sperm they join up (fertilisation), see Diagram 2, and move down the fallopian tube to the uterus (womb). The uterus is a pear-shaped hollow muscle which holds the embryo during pregnancy.

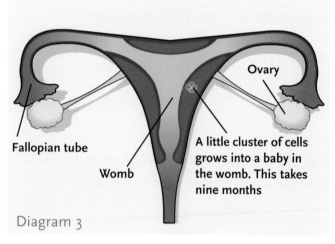

Ovary

Fallopian tube

Womb

A little cluster of cells grows into a baby in the womb. This takes nine months

Diagram 3

Pregnancy

The fertilised egg attaches itself to the wall of the womb and during the next nine months grows into a baby (pregnancy), see Diagram 3.

During the previous month the womb has been getting itself ready in case an egg is fertilised and needs nourishment. It does this by building up a spongy lining of blood vessels in the wall of the womb. The growing baby becomes attached to this by a tube called the umbilical cord. When the baby is born, this link with the mother is cut. Where it was attached to the baby becomes the navel (belly button).

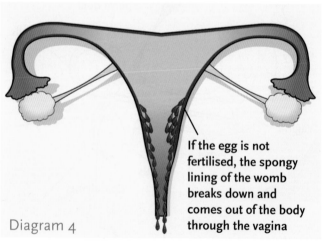

If the egg is not fertilised, the spongy lining of the womb breaks down and comes out of the body through the vagina

Diagram 4

Menstruation

If the egg does not meet a sperm and is not fertilised, no baby will be conceived that month. In this case the spongy lining of the womb won't be needed. It breaks down and comes away through the vagina (taking the unfertilised egg with it) as a trickle of blood. This is called menstruation or 'having a period', see Diagram 4.

When this happens the blood is soaked up by a sanitary towel which the girl attaches to her underwear. As a girl gets older, or is involved in sports, she may find it easier to use tampons (a tightly packed tube of cotton wool which is placed in the vagina) instead of sanitary towels.

Some interesting facts!

 There is no 'right' time at which a girl starts her periods. It can be any time between ten and sixteen years of age. The average age is around twelve or thirteen years. (If you are worried about this ask your parents/guardian, older sister or a trusted adult. They will all understand!)

 A period usually lasts between four and six days.

 The length of time between one period and the next is called the menstrual cycle. This can vary from twenty-one to forty-two days. The average is twenty-eight days. Periods can be very irregular in the beginning, but they soon settle down to a regular pattern.

 Keep a sanitary towel with you in your schoolbag. Be prepared!

 Periods continue each month until a woman reaches middle age, when they stop. This is called the menopause. They also stop when a woman is pregnant.

 Ovulation (release of the egg from the ovary) usually takes place fourteen days before the next period starts. The days just before and after the egg is released are called 'the fertile period'.

 Once the egg is released it can sometimes live for up to 48 hours.

 Sometimes, before and for the first day or two of your period, a girl may feel cramps in her tummy, or feel a little 'off form' (emotional or irritable). This is known as pre-menstrual tension (PMT). This is normal, so no need to worry!

 Puberty in boys usually starts a little later than in girls.

 Sometimes when a boy is asleep, ejaculation (release of sperm) may happen without him being aware of it. This is called a 'wet dream' and is perfectly normal.

 Sometimes during puberty a boy may have an erection for no particular reason. This shows that he is becoming an adult and is nothing to worry about.

 Sperm cells can live for up to five to seven days.

 If you are concerned about anything ask your parents, older brother or a trusted adult. They will understand!

Age of consent

In Ireland it is illegal for anyone to have sex with someone who is under the age of seventeen years. This is called the 'age of consent'. This law is there to protect young people. Even though your body may be physically ready to have sex this does not mean that you are ready emotionally (feelings) or psychologically (in your mind).

Useful Websites

www.kidshealth.org – offers honest and accurate information and advice about health, emotions and life in general for teenagers

www.girlshealth.gov – a site aimed at girls, offering information and advice on all aspects of growing up

www.cyh.com – has lots of information for teenagers on health, wellbeing and having fun

Assessment – Check your learning

With another student write or draw the story telling the journey of the egg in one box, and the journey of the sperm in the other. Then complete the crossword on the opposite page to see if you can remember the parts of the reproductive systems.

Journey of the egg

Journey of the sperm

Crossword – the reproductive systems

Clues

Across

1 Builds up on the inside of the womb, preparing it to receive a fertilised egg. If the egg is not fertilised it is released from the womb as a trickle of blood. (6, 2, 3, 4)

2 The neck of the womb through which the baby passes during birth. (6)

3 A spongy organ that expands and contracts. A lot of blood vessels run through it. It has an opening at the top that carries urine and semen from the body. (5)

4 A narrow tube going from the bladder through the penis to the outside. It carries urine and semen from the body. (7)

Down

1 There are two of these. They store eggs, one of which matures and is released each month. (7)

2 The narrow tubes through which the egg passes on the way to the uterus (womb) from the ovary. (9, 5)

3 A muscular tube connecting the womb or uterus to the outside of the body. Penis is inserted here during sexual intercourse and a baby is born through it. (6)

4 Pear-shaped hollow muscle which holds the embryo during pregnancy. (6)

5 A sac-like pouch of wrinkly tissue that holds the testes. Sperm is made in the testes. (7)

6 A muscular bag that holds urine. (7)

7 A narrow tube which carries sperm from the testes to the urethra. (5, 4)

Review of Unit 2: *Sexuality, Gender Identity and Sexual Health: Changes at Adolescence – What's Happening Inside Your Body?*

1 In this unit I learned about _____

_____

_____

2 I think that this will help me when _____

_____

_____

3 In this unit I liked _____

_____

_____

4 In this unit I did not like _____

_____

_____

5 I would like to find out more about _____

_____

_____

6 This unit links with (name another unit in SPHE or another subject) _____

_____

_____

UNIT 3 Sexuality, Gender Identity and Sexual Health

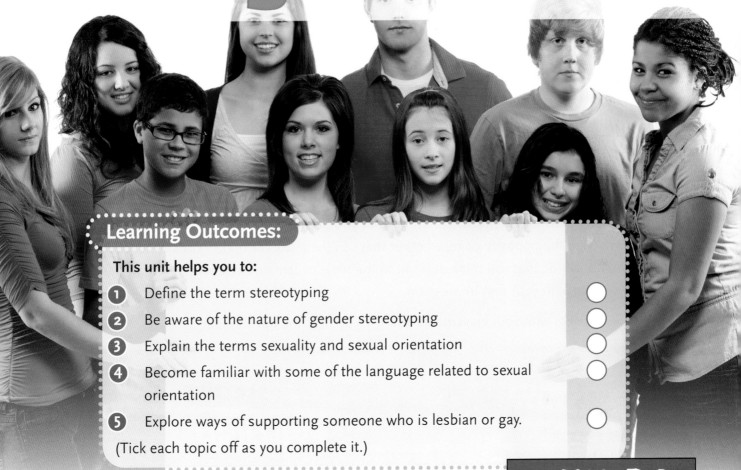

Learning Outcomes:

This unit helps you to:

1. Define the term stereotyping ⚪
2. Be aware of the nature of gender stereotyping ⚪
3. Explain the terms sexuality and sexual orientation ⚪
4. Become familiar with some of the language related to sexual orientation ⚪
5. Explore ways of supporting someone who is lesbian or gay. ⚪

(Tick each topic off as you complete it.)

Sexuality and Gender Identity

You have already explored some of the ways in which you are changing physically, socially, psychologically and emotionally as you grow through adolescence. As you mature, these changes lead you to an awareness of your sexual feelings towards other people. Sometimes you might worry about these feelings and find it hard to understand exactly why you are feeling a particular way. While this can all be quite confusing, it is a normal part of growing up and these feelings help you develop a sense of your own sexuality.

Coping with new feelings and learning about yourself can also be an exciting time. Very often your ideas and feelings can be influenced by messages you receive growing up, from your parents, family, friends, the media, the church and so on. This can be particularly true when it comes to issues of gender.

KEY WORDS

Stereotypes

Gender stereotyping

Sexuality

Sexual orientation

LGBT

Lesbian

Gay

Bisexual

Transgender

Images of male and female – gender stereotyping

Gender stereotyping means that if a person is a male or a female they are expected to live their life in a particular way, to stick to certain roles and expectations. Beliefs and expectations can come from family, society or from a specific culture or faith in which the person grows up.

This type of belief often limits a person's choices, who they are as individuals and who they might become in the future.

Let's explore this further.

KEY WORDS

Stereotype

A strongly held belief that all people or things with a particular characteristic are the same.

KEY WORDS

Gender stereotyping

This is something that people think is true about how other people look, act, think, talk or feel because they are of a certain gender. Gender stereotyping can limit who we can be and what we can do as males or females.

Activity 1 Word wall

Look at the words below and then write them in what you decide to be the most appropriate place in the Venn diagram on the opposite page, whether that's in the circle for male words or for female words. If there are words that you think don't fit in the male or female circle write them in the middle. Do it quickly and go with your first impression.

Compare your answers with your classmates and then answer the questions.

tender · VELVET · eagle · assertive · handbag · BARBIE · hurling · guns · LEATHER · weak · BUGGY · FOOTBALL · WOODWORK · COMPUTER GAMES · REMOTE · GORILLA · HOLDING HANDS · bikini · CONTROL · CUDDLING · GIFTS · DANCE · WINE · MAKE UP · texting · FACEBOOK · STRONG · Reading · SHOPPING · RIBBONS · UNDERSTANDING · MOTORBIKE · GOSSIP · Muscular · PINK · engineering · trousers · BEER · dusting · flower · Butterfly · ROUGH · SNAPCHAT

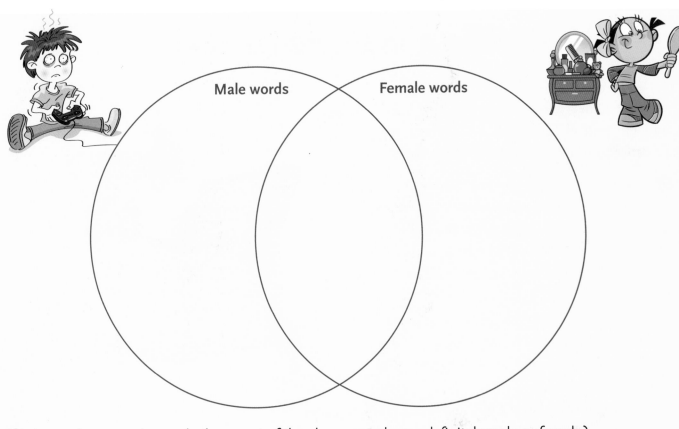

1 Were there certain words that most of the class agreed were definitely male or female?
What were they?

_____

_____

2 Were there words that you thought belonged in the middle? Why did you put those there?

_____

_____

3 How did you divide the words up?

_____

_____

4 Why might this sort of division not be good?

_____

_____

5 What does this activity tell us about how we think about men and women in terms of their
behaviour, appearance, personality and abilities?

_____

_____

6 Why is it not fair to make generalised comments about what it means to be male or female?

_____

_____

Activity 2

Act like a man/Be ladylike

We have all heard the sayings 'Act like a man!' and 'Be ladylike!'. Let's look at how these ideas can affect our relationships and behaviour.

Box A

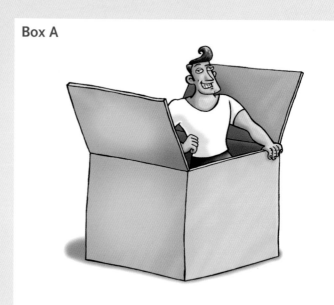

1. On the outside of box A list the things that 'acting like a man' can mean. Where do we learn these roles? Home? School? Community? Movies? Work? Write the answers to this question on the lid of the box.

2. What names do we call boys who don't fit into the box and who act differently? Write these names around box A. Why do we do this?

3. How might this affect a boy or a young man?

Box B

4. On the outside of box B list the things that 'being ladylike' can mean. Where do we learn these roles? Home? School? Community? Movies? Work? Write the answers to this question on the lid of the box.

5. What do we call girls who don't fit into the box and who want to act differently? Write these names around box B. Why do we do this?

6. How might this affect a girl or a young woman?

LEARNING LOG

An issue of gender stereotyping I'm aware of is

_____

_____

Something I can do to reduce gender stereotyping is

_____

_____

Gender Stereotyping

It is often difficult not be constrained by gender stereotypes. Sometimes it means taking a risk to 'Act outside the box'.

LGBT – Lesbian, Gay, Bisexual and Transgender

Activity 3

Match the words – what do you know?

We hear a lot about words that are to do with 'sexuality', 'sexual orientation' and 'gender identity'. But what do they actually mean? Do the activity below to find out. Your teacher will give you the correct answers.

Match the term from column A with the correct definition from column B – by drawing a line from words in A to definitions in B (one is done for you).

PowerPoint

A	B
Sexuality	Sometimes called 'Trans', this refers to someone whose gender identity differs from the one they are at birth. They may identify as male or female but don't feel comfortable as such. Some transgender people, as adults, may decide to change their gender and become transsexual.
Sexual Orientation	People who are attracted to people of the opposite sex. They are often referred to as being 'straight'. Most people are heterosexual. *Hetero* comes from the Greek word meaning 'other'.
Gender identity	A person's sense of being male, female or transgender.
Heterosexual	Who we are attracted to, whether that's people of the opposite sex, the same sex or both. It is important that we learn to respect and value the sexual identities of others in the way that we want our own sexual identity to be accepted and valued.
Homosexual	A person who is attracted to someone of the same sex. The terms for different genders most people use are lesbian, gay and bisexual.
Bisexual	A female who is attracted to other females.
Transgender	A male who is attracted to other males.
Lesbian	A person who is attracted to both women and men.
Gay	Our understanding of what it means to be male or female and how we show that in all aspects of our lives: how we dress, how we behave, who we are attracted to, who we love, the way we think and how we feel. It is personal to each one of us and is often difficult to talk about.

Did You Know?

A person does not choose his/her sexuality. You cannot tell whether someone is straight, lesbian, gay, bisexual or transgender by looking at them.

Being gay, lesbian or bisexual is different from being transgender.

Being gay, lesbian or bisexual is about who you are attracted to.

BEING TRANSGENDER IS ABOUT HOW YOU FEEL ABOUT YOUR OWN GENDER (BEING MALE OR FEMALE).

The legal age for having sex in Ireland is seventeen years old. It is the same for people of all sexual orientations.

Sexual stereotyping

The statistics below are from a 2016 report on sexual stereotyping, *The LGBT Ireland Report: national study of the mental health and wellbeing of lesbian, gay, bisexual, transgender and intersex people in Ireland.*

- Only 20 per cent of LGBT students felt they really belonged in their school
- Only 44 per cent said they were positively affirmed in their school
- Half of the LGBT young people surveyed personally experienced anti-LGBT bullying
- Over two-thirds (67 per cent) of LGBT students witnessed bullying of other LGBT students in their school
- One in four LGBT students missed school to avoid being negatively treated
- One in four LGBT students considered leaving school early
- One in twenty LGBT students did leave school early.

Research has also found that the most common age that young people say they became aware that they were gay/lesbian is when they were twelve years old. But the most common age when they told someone else they were gay/lesbian was seventeen. As in the statistics above, some students felt very unsafe in school and found it so difficult to cope that they left early.

Assessment A – Check your learning

How can *YOU* help?

It is coming to the end of the summer holidays and you are about to start second year. Your friend, who has been away for most of the summer, emails you to say he/she is gay and hasn't been able to tell anyone. Your friend is not looking forward to coming back to school as other gay students have been bullied and hassled in the past. One in particular, in third year, has had comments posted on Facebook about them.

Think about your friend and how they are feeling returning to school. Write down four things you can do or say to support them when you all go back to school.

1 _____

2 _____

3 _____

4 _____

OR

Assessment B – Check your learning

Changing roles

Over the years the roles and what is expected of men and women in society has changed a lot. Interview two or three older people in your community – parents, grandparents and others – to find out exactly how things have changed and the effects of these changes on men and women today. Make out your interview questions and carry out your interviews, orally or in writing. In either case, keep a record of your questions and responses in your SPHE folder or e-folder.

Something new that I learned about stereotyping is _____

_____

Something I'm more aware of about sexuality is _____

_____

As a result of this I will _____

_____

LEARNING LOG

Useful Websites

www.belongto.org – an organisation for lesbian, gay, bisexual and transgender young people

www.barnardos.ie/teenhelp – provides support, help and advice to teenagers, as part of Barnardos' aim to make Ireland a safer place for children

www.childline.ie – provides support to children and teenagers up to 18 years of age

Review of Unit 3: *Sexuality, Gender Identity and Sexual Health*

1. In this unit I learned about _____

   _____

   _____

2. I think that this will help me when _____

   _____

   _____

3. In this unit I liked _____

   _____

   _____

4. In this unit I did not like _____

   _____

   _____

5. I would like to find out more about _____

   _____

   _____

6. This unit links with (name another unit in SPHE or another subject) _____

   _____

   _____

UNIT 1 Positive Mental Health

Learning Outcomes:

This unit helps you to:

1. Understand what it means to have positive mental health ○
2. Appreciate the importance of talking things over and getting help ○
3. Recognise the link between thoughts, feelings and behaviour. ○

(Tick each topic off as you complete it.)

> **KEY WORDS**
>
> Positive mental health
>
> **Feelings**

Positive mental health includes:

Having the skills for getting along with people in your life

Good self-confidence and self-esteem

Knowing how to cope with stress in your life and deal with tough times

Being able to ask for help and knowing where to get it

Knowing what you are feeling and how to express those feelings in a healthy way

> **KEY WORDS**
>
> Positive mental health
>
> Having a sense of self-esteem and wellbeing, being able to solve problems, to deal with stress and manage your feelings.

Emotional health is an important part of positive mental health. To have good mental health a person needs:

- To be aware of their emotions (feelings)
- To be able to express these feelings properly
- To manage their emotions so that negative emotions, such as depression, stress, anxiety, fear and anger, do not take over their life.

We will look at this in greater detail on pages 171 to 182.

Did You Know?

Most young people grow up with good mental and emotional health but surveys tell us that more adolescents have mental health problems now than thirty years ago.

REMEMBER

In this unit we will be covering a variety of sensitive issues. Some students might find these topics difficult to talk about. You, or others in your class, may be affected personally by the topic that we are discussing, or you may know someone else who has been affected by it. Please be respectful and thoughtful of others, and treat the subject responsibly. Remember your SPHE Ground Rules.

Recognising positive mental health

In Strand Two we looked at what physical health and mental health mean. Some people may have good physical health but rate poorly for positive mental/emotional health and vice versa.

The following case study on Joanne O'Riordan from Millstreet, County Cork, gives us a good insight into positive mental health. When you have access to the internet you can get more background information on her life.

Activity

1

No Limbs No Limits

Read the information below and then out of ten rate Joanne's physical health and then her positive mental health.

Joanne O'Riordan is one of only seven living people born with Total Amelia, a syndrome where people are born with no arms or legs. She has campaigned worldwide for the rights of people with disabilities and has successfully forced the Irish government into a U-turn on disability cuts. Joanne addressed the United Nations on her sixteenth birthday, and has discussed the development of technology to aid her disability with the Massachusetts Institute of Technology (MIT) and Apple. As a consequence, engineers at Trinity College, Dublin are developing 'Robbie the Robot' to assist Joanne with her daily life.

She was named Cork Person of the Month and Young Person of the Year 2012 at the People of the Year Awards. In 2014 she enrolled in UCC to study criminology. In 2015 Joanne was awarded one of only ten Junior Chamber International's (JCI) Outstanding Young Person of the World awards and in 2016 she was the youngest ever Grand Marshall to lead the St Patrick's Festival parade in Dublin.

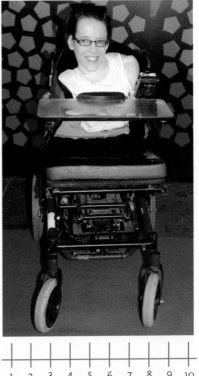

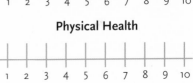

Physical Health

| 1 | 2 | 3 | 4 | 5 | 6 | 7 | 8 | 9 | 10 |

Mental/Emotional Health

1 = Poor Health
10 = Excellent Health

1 What challenges does Joanne O'Riordan face?

_____

_____

_____

_____

2 How well does she deal with these challenges?

_____

_____

_____

_____

3 What does Joanne's story tell us about the importance of positive mental health in our lives?

_____

_____

_____

_____

Activity 2 — The great debate

Look back at the definitions of positive mental health and physical health (Strand 2, page 49). In your class arrange a debate on the topic: 'Mental health is more important than physical health.' Get into teams of four.

Your teacher will tell you whether you are **for** (support) or **against** (oppose) the **motion** (topic). As a group write your team's speech and choose a spokesperson to present your argument to the class. Pick a judging panel of three students to mark each team.

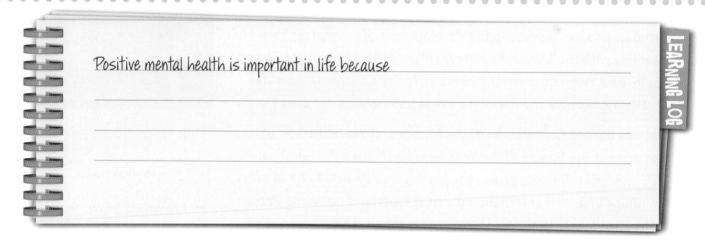

Positive mental health is important in life because _____

LEARNING LOG

Maintaining positive mental health

Maintaining positive mental health can be a bit of a balancing act and even in a single day most people can feel up and down and have mood swings. Sometimes, especially during your teenage years, you can have longer spells of feeling down in the dumps. This is perfectly normal but it is important to be aware of when you are feeling low. You also need to remember that there are things you can do to make yourself feel better so that you are able to get on with enjoying your life.

Activity 3 — Walking the line

Look at the image on the opposite page. In the clouds write all of the things that can knock a person, of any age, off balance.

Along the balance pole write all of the actions that help to keep you balanced.

On the space between the steps of the ladder, name all of the actions and people that can help you to get back up when you have a knock or lose your balance.

This activity can be done on your own first, then pool your ideas with two other students in your class. Nominate a spokesperson to feed your group's findings back to the whole class.

Talking Things Over and Getting Help

Remember, everyone has ups and downs. That's life. What's important is that you know when you need help and where to get it. It is especially important when you are a teenager, with all of the changes that are going on in your life and in your family's life, that you know where to turn to for help if you need it.

Activity 4

What would you do?

Think about one of the scenarios below and, in pairs, answer the questions that follow to help you to work out what might be done to help. Your teacher will tell you which one you are to work on.

Jessica is thirteen years old and life at home is not good. Her parents either argue all the time or do not talk to each other at all. Jessica is finding it difficult to concentrate and her school grades are going down. She hasn't told anyone and feels sad all of the time.

Amal is thirteen years old and studying for his summer exams. The classes will be divided into Higher and Ordinary level next year on the basis of results in some subjects. His parents are expecting that he will do well and have high hopes for him. Amal is so anxious that he is not able to concentrate and can't take in the material he is studying.

Jenny is fourteen years old. She used to play some sports in primary school but since she went into first year she has to catch the school bus in the afternoons, so she has dropped out of games. She has put on a lot of weight and doesn't seem to be able to do anything about it. The school uniform covers it up a bit but in her ordinary clothes she feels very self-conscious about her body. Jenny has stopped going out and her friends don't ask her to do things any more.

Animation

1 How do you think s/he is feeling?

_____

_____

2 How might things be better if s/he got help?

_____

_____

_____

3 What do you think s/he could do to get help?

_____

_____

_____

4 Why might s/he be afraid to ask for help?

_____

_____

_____

5 What advice would you give to him/her?

_____

_____

_____

Asking for help – top tips to remember

- It is not a sign of weakness to ask for help
- Everybody needs help at some time in his or her life
- Tell someone if you have a problem, before it gets too big to handle
- Learn how to talk about how you are feeling
- Be open about listening to advice from people you trust, such as your friends or family
- Think about what might happen if you don't ask for help
- Think of how things could improve if you do seek help
- Think about how you can help others with their problems
- Learn about the different help agencies.

Getting Help

Apart from family and friends, you can get help from many different organisations and agencies. Below are the contact details for some help agencies.

Childline
A round-the-clock service for children and adolescents seeking confidential help.
www.childline.ie
Freephone: 1800 666 666

Samaritans
A 24-hour service offering a listening ear and confidential help to anybody in difficulty or crisis.
www.samaritans.org
Freephone: 116123

BeLonG To
A support group for lesbian, gay, bisexual and transgender young people between the ages of fourteen to twenty-three years.
www.belongto.org

CARI: Children at Risk Ireland
Provides support and counselling for children and families affected by sexual abuse.
www.cari.ie
Helpline: 1890 924 567

Aware
A helpline offering help and support to people who suffer from depression. Also runs support groups around the country for individuals and their families.
www.aware.ie
Freephone: 1800 80 48 48

Alateen
Provides support to anyone whose life is being or has been affected by someone else's drinking.
www.al-anon-ireland.org
Tel: 01 8732699 Helpline

TeenLine Ireland
A freephone service offering support for teenagers who feel alone, worried, depressed or for those who just need to talk to someone confidentially.
www.teenline.ie
Freephone: 1800 833 634

Teen Between
A support service offered to young people between the ages of twelve and twenty-one years whose parents have separated or divorced, or are separating or going through a divorce.
www.teenbetween.ie

HeadsUp
A text-messaging support service that helps young people to deal with their problems before these get too big. HeadsUp supplies a list of help numbers related to your particular difficulty.
Text 'Headsup' to 50424

Rainbows Ireland
An organisation that provides peer-support programmes for people of all ages who have experienced death, separation or divorce of someone in their lives.
www.rainbowsireland.ie
Tel: 01 473 4175

ReachOut Ireland
An online youth mental health service to help young people get through tough times.
www.reachout.com

Bodywhys
An organisation that offers support to people affected by eating disorders.
www.bodywhys.ie
Tel: 1890 200 444

Activity 5

Who can help?

1 Select one of the agencies mentioned on page 160, or another agency that you know about, which offers help and support to young people, and research and prepare a short presentation for your class about the help and support it offers. You can keep this in your SPHE folder or your e-folder.

Use the pointers below to describe the work of this organisation. Feel free to include anything else that you think is important. Keep your log in your SPHE folder.

(a) Why would someone contact them?

(b) What sort of help do they offer?

(c) How can you contact them, e.g. phone number, website, opening hours?

(d) What might happen if you contact them?

2 State which agencies you think might be able to help Jessica, Amal and Jenny with their difficulties.

Jessica:_____

Amal:_____

Jenny:_____

LEARNING LOG

Would you be happy to contact an agency for help? If yes, explain why. If no, explain why not.

_____

If I asked someone for help, I would expect _____

_____

_____

Emotional Health: Feelings

Being able to identify, talk about and manage your feelings is a big part of positive mental and emotional health. This is really important so that you get on well with your family and friends. Not knowing how to express your emotions can make you feel upset and unhappy and can make it difficult for other people to get on with you.

Recognising feelings

It is important that you learn to identify the most common feelings and look at healthy ways of expressing them so that they don't build up inside you and cause you trouble. For example, if you are dropped from a team it is normal to feel disappointed that you were not selected.

Sometimes you might not recognise that you are disappointed and simply mistake the feeling for anger at the selector or resentment against the player who got your place. While feeling disappointed might spur you on to train harder, feeling angry and full of resentment can cause you to dislike yourself or to put the blame for what's happening to you onto others. This is not good.

KEY WORDS

Feelings

An emotional state or reaction. A feeling word describes how you react to an event, situation or person. Emotions is another word for feelings.

Remember feelings are neither good nor bad, it's how we manage them that matters!

Activity 6

Snow White and the Seven Dwarfs

Using what you have already learned about facial expression and body language, write the correct names of each of the seven dwarfs below. Choose from the following list:

Sad, Frightened, Grumpy, Proud, Angry, Surprised, Disappointed, Nervous, Confused, Bashful, Happy, Scared.

1 _____
2 _____
3 _____
4 _____
5 _____
6 _____
7 _____

1 What clues in the faces and body language helped you to decide the names of the dwarfs?

_____

_____

2 Which were the easiest and why?

_____

3 Were there ones that you found difficult?

_____

4 Which ones?

_____

5 Were these the same for the other students in your group/class?

_____

6 Apart from a person's face (facial expressions) and body language, are there any other clues that tell you how someone is feeling?

_____

_____

Activity 7 My feelings

Look at the feelings poster. Choose four of the less common feelings and complete the following sentences about each of them.

1 I felt _____ when _____

_____

_____

2 I felt _____ when _____

_____

_____

3 I felt _____ when _____

4 I felt _____ when _____

_____

nervous	frightened	ashamed	guilty
ecstatic	confident	shy	proud
embarrassed	overwhelmed	enraged	depressed

Four basic feelings

Our facial expressions, body language and tone of voice often show how we feel. There are four basic feelings that we experience in different situations. These are **sad**, **angry**, **happy** and **scared**. All feelings can be placed in one or more of these categories.

Activity 8

Feeling your way

Look at the feeling words used in Activity 7 and place them under one or more of the headings below. An example would be 'Frightened'. This is a scared feeling so it should go under the 'Scared' heading. Sometimes when you are frightened you could also be sad so you could also write it under the 'Sad' heading.

Angry	Sad	Happy	Scared

Something new that I learned about feelings in this lesson is _____

_____

_____

Something new that I learned about myself is _____

_____

_____

LEARNING LOG

9 Measuring your feelings

We can represent the way we feel in different situations on a feelings thermometer. Look at the feelings thermometers below, representing each of the four basic feelings.

Angry   **Sad**   **Happy**   **Scared**

Read the ten statements below and pick a feeling for each statement. Decide which of the four thermometers you want to use for this feeling and write the name of the feeling on the point of the thermometer you think it belongs to and mark it with the number of the statement. For example, if you feel delighted when school is finished write 'delighted' near the top (or right at the top!) of the Happy feelings thermometer and write number 1 beside it because it is the first statement.

1. How I feel when school finishes.

2. How I feel when I am with my friends.

3. How I feel when I am dropped from my team.

4. How I feel when I have an argument at home.

5. How I feel when I have to give an answer in class.

6. How I feel when I do well in a test.

7. How I feel when someone posts something good about me online.

8. How I feel when I do not have my work done for class.

9. How I feel relaxing, watching TV or listening to music.

10. How I feel when I am sick.

Respecting my feelings and the feelings of others

Let's look at how we can express and manage our feelings in a way that is respectful to ourselves and to others. By doing so, we also learn how to understand other people's feelings and deal with disagreements and conflicts.

We can often guess what people feel from their facial expressions and their body language. If people find it hard to express what they are feeling, we need to know how to ask them. We also need to be careful of the words that we use in these situations.

· · · · · **Activity** ·

10 | How do they feel?

Look at the four pictures below in which someone is experiencing strong feelings. Examine each picture and with a partner answer the questions beside each one.

1 What do think is going on in the picture? How do you know?

2 How do you think they feel (use several words)?

3 If you were in that scene with them what would you do?

4 What would you say to them?

1 _____

2 _____

3 _____

4 _____
_____

1 _____

2 _____

3 _____

4 _____
_____

1 _____

2 _____

3 _____

4 _____

_____

1 _____

2 _____

3 _____

4 _____

_____

Sometimes it's difficult to talk about how you feel. It can also be hard to listen to other people talking about how they feel.

It's important for your positive mental health that you learn how to be more comfortable in these situations. The first step is to learn how to express how you feel.

Activity 11 — Owning my feelings

Read the six sentences below. For each feeling word, complete the sentence to describe a situation when you felt like that.

1 I felt **strong** when _____

2 I felt **sad** when _____

3 I felt **happy** when _____

4 I felt **sympathetic** when _____

5 I felt **angry** when _____

6 I felt **proud** when _____

Two things I learned about myself while doing these activities are:

1 _____

2 _____

_____

Hint: Did you find it easy or difficult to do the activities? Why do you think you found it easy/difficult? Did you like doing them – why/why not? _____

The link between thoughts, feelings and behaviour

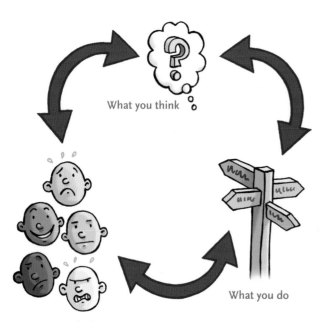

What you think

How you feel

What you do

What we **think** about something can change how we **feel** about it and how we then **act** or behave. This can go on and on and become a vicious cycle. For example, if your parent asks you to do something like tidying your room, you might **think** that they are picking on you unfairly and you **feel** annoyed so you rudely answer them back (**behaviour**). This makes them **feel** angry and they may react by snapping at you which convinces you that they are totally unreasonable people altogether and you feel really unlucky to have them as parents so you snap back at them. This cycle can go on and on!

To break the cycle, you need to change how you are thinking. So if your parent asks you to tidy your room, instead of getting angry, you **think** 'That's fair enough, it's in a bit of a state but I want to finish this game first' so you say: 'OK, I'll do it – can I finish up this game first?' They **think** you are being fairly reasonable and **feel** happy about that so they say: 'That's fine, thanks.' You **feel** less annoyed and chances are you will put more effort into tidying up your room (**act**), as you are feeling less hard done by.

Thought

Feeling

Behaviour

Assessment – Check your learning

In Example A below fill in the thought, feeling and behaviour bubbles to show the effect of negative thoughts. Then in Example B show how the outcome can change when the negative thought is replaced with a positive one.

Scan your work and save it to your SPHE e-folder.

Thought, feeling and behaviour

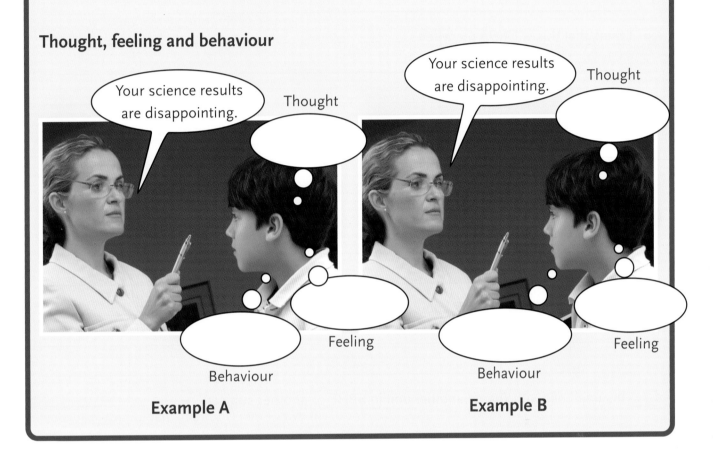

Example A

Example B

One example in my own life where changing how I thought about something changed the outcome is

LEARNING LOG

Review of Unit 1: *Positive Mental Health*

1 In this unit I learned about _____

_____

_____

2 I think that this will help me when _____

_____

_____

3 In this unit I liked _____

_____

_____

4 In this unit I did not like _____

_____

_____

5 I would like to find out more about _____

_____

_____

6 This unit links with (name another unit in SPHE or another subject) _____

_____

_____

UNIT 2 Dealing with Tough Times

KEY WORDS

Mental wellbeing

Resilience

Mindfulness

Relaxation response

Pressures on Young People

Young people may experience a lot of pressures during their teenage years. It can be hard for them to cope and keep a sense of wellbeing.

Did You Know?

About 20 per cent of the world's children and adolescents have mental disorders or problems. About half of the mental disorders begin before the age of fourteen.

Wellbeing

The World Health Organization (WHO) defines student wellbeing as the student being aware of his or her abilities, being able to manage the stresses in their life, enjoying learning and feeling that he or she belongs to a community.

Good mental wellbeing is not just about having good or happy things in your life but it is also about being able to manage the issues and problems that are part of your life. Being able to manage the ups and downs of life is also called resilience.

KEY WORDS

Resilience

The capacity to deal with change and challenges and to bounce back after difficulties in your life.

Five a day for mental wellbeing

There are five steps which most experts agree we can all take to help our mental wellbeing. Why don't you try them out and see for yourself?

1 **Connect** – (Relationships) Get to know the people around you and make a link with them: your family, friends, classmates, teammates and neighbours. Spend time building and minding these relationships.

2 **Be active** – You don't have to be a super athlete to be active. Take a walk, go cycling or play a game of football. Find an activity in school or where you live that you enjoy and make it a part of your life.

3 **Keep learning** – (Keep your brain alive) Learning new skills can give you a sense of achievement and a new confidence. So why not try to do something new after school, start learning to play a musical instrument or go to a summer camp?

4 **Give to others** – You may have heard of Random Acts of Kindness – even the smallest random act can count, whether it's a smile, a thank you or a kind word.

Bigger things such as volunteering in your local community or helping out at school, can improve your mental wellbeing and help you build new friendships and connections.

5 **Take notice** – (Be mindful) Be more aware of the present moment, including your feelings and thoughts, and of your body and the world around you. Some people call this awareness 'mindfulness', and it can really make a positive change to the way you feel about life and how you approach challenges.

 **PowerPoint**

It's our struggles which make us strong

'The strongest oak of the forest is not the one that is protected from the storm and hidden from the sun. It's the one that stands in the open where it is compelled to struggle for its existence against the winds and rains and the scorching sun.'

Napoleon Hill (1883–1970)

LEARNING LOG

One thing I am doing well to make me more resilient is

The area I need to work on to improve my resilience is

Relaxation Techniques

In this section we are going to look at relaxation techniques and how you can use them to help you deal with stress in your life. For many of us, relaxation means chilling out in front of the TV at the end of a busy day. But watching TV does little to get rid of stress.

To fight stress properly, you need to set off the body's **natural relaxation response**. You can do this by practising relaxation techniques such as deep breathing, meditation, rhythmic exercise and yoga. Making time for these activities in your life can help to reduce your everyday stress and boost your energy and improve your mood.

KEY WORDS

Relaxation responses

A state of deep calmness that is the opposite of the stress response. It is your ability to manage your own body so that it releases chemicals which make your muscles and organs slow down while increasing the blood flow to your brain. This relaxes you and helps you to feel less stressed.

How do you get the relaxation response?

A variety of different relaxation techniques can produce the relaxation response but it can't be achieved by lying on the couch or sleeping. The technique you use needs to be a mentally active process that leaves your body and your mind relaxed, calm and focused.

Learning the basics of these relaxation techniques isn't difficult, but it does take practice. Most experts recommend that you practise for 10–20 minutes each day. If this seems like a lot, remember that you can carry out many of these techniques while you are at your desk or on the bus/in the car coming or going to school.

There is no single technique that is best for everyone. Below are the most common ones. Try them out by practising them for a few weeks so you can see which ones work best for you.

Breathing meditation

With its focus on full, cleansing breaths, deep breathing is a simple, yet powerful, relaxation technique. It is the cornerstone of many other relaxation practices too. It's easy to learn, can be practised almost anywhere, and is a quick way to get your stress levels in check. All you really need is a few minutes and a place where you can relax.

1 Sixty second breathing meditation

Tune into your breathing at different times during the day, focus on it and follow the steps below:

1 Breathe in through your nose on a count of four seconds.

2 Hold that breath for seven seconds.

3 Exhale slowly through your mouth on a count of eight seconds.

Repeat steps 1–3 three times.

Become aware of your thoughts and feelings at these moments, just be conscious of them, without judging them or yourself. Note them . . . and then let them go.

Mindfulness

In a practical way mindfulness is simply making sure that you notice thoughts, physical sensations, sights, sounds, smells – anything you might not normally notice. The actual skills might be simple, but because 'being mindful' is so different to how our minds normally behave, it takes a lot of practice to do it.

For example, while your mam might go into the garden, look around and think, 'That grass really needs cutting, and that vegetable patch looks terrible,' your younger brother will be shouting, 'Come and look at this ant!'. They are both looking at the same thing but are seeing it in two completely different ways.

If you are being mindful you should see things that you wouldn't normally notice – because your head is usually too busy thinking about something you need to do in the future or going over what you have already done in the past.

Mindfulness might simply be described as choosing and learning to control what you are going to pay attention to and living in the present.

> ### KEY WORDS
>
> **Mindfulness**
>
> An ancient practice that is a very simple concept. It is so simple that it can be difficult to explain! Mindfulness means paying attention in a particular way and really staying in the present moment and not worrying about what's past or what's to come in the future.

Mindful breathing

The main focus in mindfulness meditation is your breathing. When you practise mindfulness (and it does take practice) you allow thoughts and feelings to come and go without getting caught up in them. This creates a sense of calmness and acceptance.

To try this out follow the steps below:

1   Sit comfortably, with your eyes closed and your spine reasonably straight.

2   Direct your attention to your breathing.

3   When thoughts, emotions, physical feelings or outside sounds occur, simply accept them, giving them the space to come and go without getting involved with them.

4   When you notice that your attention has drifted off and is becoming caught up in thoughts or feelings about the past or future, simply note that your attention has drifted, and then gently bring it back to your breathing and on being in the moment.

It's okay and natural for thoughts to arise, and for your attention to follow those thoughts. No matter how many times this happens, just keep bringing the focus of your attention back to your breathing.

Activity

2 Practising mindfulness and breathing meditation

1   Find a comfortable position lying on your back or sitting up. If you are sitting, keep your spine straight and let your shoulders drop.

2   Close your eyes if it feels comfortable.

3   Bring your attention to your tummy, feeling it rise or expand gently on the in-breath and flatten on the out-breath.

4   Keep your focus on your breathing, concentrate on each in-breath for its full duration and on each out-breath for its full duration, as if you were riding the waves of your own breathing.

5   Every time you notice that your mind has wandered off the breath gently bring your attention back to your tummy and the feeling of the breath coming in and out. If your mind wanders away from the breath 10 times, then your job is simply to bring the focus of your attention back to the breath every time, no matter what your mind becomes preoccupied with.

6   Practise this exercise for fifteen minutes at a convenient time every day, whether you feel like it or not, for one week and see how it feels to incorporate a disciplined meditation practice into your life. Be aware of how it feels to spend some time each day just *being with* your breath without having to *do anything*.

Visualisation or guided imagery

Visualisation, or guided imagery, is a type of meditation where you use not only your eyes, but also your senses of taste, touch, smell and sound. To use it as a relaxation technique you need to imagine a scene where you feel at peace and free to let go of all tension and worry. Choose whatever setting you find most calming, whether it's a sunny beach, a favourite room at home or a quiet wood.

You can do this visualisation meditation on your own in silence, or while listening to soothing music. To help you to use your sense of hearing you can download sounds that match your chosen setting, for example you could have the sound of ocean waves playing in the background if you've chosen a beach.

Did You Know?

Visualisation, or guided imagery, is considered to be more effective as a meditation technique if you practise it regularly. It can be used to:

- Help you to relax
- Meditate
- Improve your exam performance
- Help you to gain confidence
- Improve your mood
- Reduce distress associated with upsetting memories
- Assist in overcoming physical illnesses
- Improve sports performance.

How does visualisation work?

Start each visualisation session with relaxation, by getting comfortable in a quiet place where you won't be disturbed and taking a couple of minutes to focus on your breathing and the scene you've chosen. Close your eyes, then mentally check your body and take note of any area where there is tension. Let that tension go with each out-breath.

All visualisations work better if you use all your senses in building the picture in your mind's eye – it's more than just seeing! If you are imagining walking on a beach, you can smell the sea and the seaweed, hear the seagulls calling, feel the sand under your bare feet, taste the salt on your lips and see the waves rolling in from the horizon.

If you notice any negative images entering your 'good' scene, then leave that image and think of something else.

Finish each visualisation by taking a few moments to bring yourself back into the room you are in, opening your eyes and looking around, sitting up, and slowly bringing yourself back to the 'here and now'.

Relaxing 'safe place' imagery

Imagine a place where you can feel calm, peaceful and safe. It may be a place you've been to before, somewhere you've dreamt about going to or maybe somewhere you've seen a picture of.

Using this 'safe place' imagery can help you if you are upset, unsure or frightened. Your image becomes linked with good feelings and can help you to calm yourself and manage your stress or anxiety.

Activity 3

Feeling safe

It's important to practise imagining or creating your 'safe place'. Take your time doing this and make the idea of it in your mind – the feel, smell, sounds – as complete as possible. This will make it easier for you to think of your safe place when you may need it to help you to reduce the feeling of stress in your life.

Think of a safe place. Focus on the colours in your peaceful and safe place.

Now notice the sounds that are around you or perhaps the silence.

Think about any smells you notice there.

Then focus on any skin sensations – the earth beneath you, the temperature, any movement of air, anything else you can touch.

While you're in your peaceful and safe place, you might choose to give it a name, whether one word or a phrase, that you can use to bring that image back, any time you need to.

You can choose to linger in your safe place a while, just enjoying the peacefulness and serenity. You can leave whenever you want to, just by opening your eyes and slowly becoming aware of where you are now.

Personal reflection: On your own, check how easy it was to think up your 'safe place'.

What helped you to do it? _____

What made it difficult? _____

Progressive muscle relaxation exercise

Progressive muscle relaxation is an exercise where you relax your mind and body by progressively tensing and relaxing muscle groups throughout your entire body. To do it right you need to tense each muscle group firmly, for about five seconds, but without straining, and then suddenly release the tension and feel the muscle relax. If you have any pain or discomfort in any of the targeted muscle groups, feel free to leave out that muscle.

As you are doing the activity below try to visualise or imagine your muscles tensing and a wave of relaxation flowing over them as you release that tension.

Activity

4 Progressive muscle relaxation

It is important that you keep to a fixed breathing pattern throughout this exercise. Take a long, deep breath in, while you tense the muscle group, and breathe out as you relax. As you breathe, notice your stomach rising and your lungs filling with air.

Now let's begin.

Start by finding a comfortable position either sitting or lying down in a place where you will not be interrupted. If you are doing this at home, you can lie flat on your bed and it will help you to sleep. Your clothes should be loose and comfortable.

Keep your attention on your body. If you begin to notice your mind wandering, bring it back to the muscle you are working on.

Take a deep breath and feel your tummy rising, hold for about five seconds, and breathe out slowly. As you exhale, imagine the tension in your body being released and flowing out of your body.

And again inhale – and exhale. Feel your body already relaxing.

As you go through each step on pages 180–181, remember to keep to this breathing pattern.

1 Tighten the muscles in your forehead by raising your eyebrows as high as you can. Hold for about five seconds. And abruptly release, feeling that tension fall away.

> **Pause for about 10 seconds and breathe.**

2 Smile widely, feeling your mouth and cheeks tense. Hold for about 5 seconds, and release, noticing the softness in your face.

> **Pause for about 10 seconds and breathe.**

3 Tighten your eye muscles by squinting your eyelids tightly shut. Hold for about 5 seconds, and let go.

> **Pause for about 10 seconds and breathe.**

4 Gently pull your head back as if to look at the ceiling. Stop if you feel any discomfort here. Hold for about 5 seconds, and release, feeling the tension ease away.

> **Pause for about 10 seconds.**
>
> **Breathe in – and out.**
>
> **In – and out.**
>
> **Let go of all the stress.**
>
> In – and out.

5 Tightly, but without straining, clench your fists and hold this position for 5 seconds, and slowly release while breathing out.

> **Pause for about 10 seconds and breathe.**

6 Bringing up your fists to your shoulders, flex your biceps. Feel that build-up of tension. Hold for about 5 seconds, and release. Notice the release.

> **Breathe in – and out.**

7 Tighten your triceps by extending your arms out and locking your elbows. Hold for about 5 seconds, and release, breathing out slowly.

> **Pause for about 10 seconds and breathe.**

8 Lift your shoulders up, as if they could touch your ears. Hold for about 5 seconds, and quickly release, feeling their heaviness.

> **Pause for about 10 seconds and breathe.**

9 Tense your upper back by pulling your shoulders back trying to make your shoulder blades touch. Hold for about 5 seconds, and breathe out and release.

> **Pause for about 10 seconds and breathe.**

10 Tighten your chest by taking a deep breath in, hold for about 5 seconds, and exhale, blowing out all the tension.

11 Now tighten the muscles in your stomach by sucking in. Hold for about 5 seconds, and release.

> **Pause for about 10 seconds and breathe.**

12 Gently arch your lower back while breathing in. Hold for about 5 seconds, breathe out and relax.

> **Pause for about 10 seconds and breathe.**
>
> **Breathe in – and out.**

13 Feel the relaxation in your upper body letting go of the tension and stress, hold for about 5 seconds, and breathe out.

14 Tighten your buttocks. Hold for about 5 seconds, and release, imagine your hips falling loose.

> **Pause for about 10 seconds and breathe.**

15 Tighten your thighs by pressing your knees together. Hold for about 5 seconds, and release.

> **Pause for about 10 seconds and breathe.**

16 Now flex your feet, pulling your toes up towards you and feeling the tension in your calves. Hold for about 5 seconds, and relax, feel the weight of your legs sinking down.

> **Pause for about 10 seconds and breathe.**

17 Curl your toes under, tensing your feet. Hold for about 5 seconds, and release.

> **Pause for about 10 seconds and breathe.**

18 Now imagine a wave of relaxation slowly spreading through your body, beginning at your head and going all the way down to your feet.

Feel the weight of your relaxed body.

> **Breathe in – and out, in – and out, in – and out.**

It's important to practise progressive muscle relaxation often, whether you are feeling anxious or not. This will make the exercise even more effective when you really do need to relax! Though it may feel a bit of a chore at first, in time you will gain a skill that will probably become a very important part of managing your anxiety in your daily life.

REMEMBER

Remember – Don't Bottle Things Up!

The worst thing you can do is to bottle up your problems, worries or stresses and tell no one about them. You may think that your problem or worry is only happening to you, but in fact one in five young people (aged 12–25) are going through a tough time at any one moment. Of these, only a tiny minority are receiving professional or voluntary help. So if you are going through a bad time you're not alone, and you don't have to keep it to yourself.

While it is always good to talk to a trusted adult at home or in school, if you don't want to do that the list of websites on page 160 will give you information and help on mental wellbeing issues.

Did You Know?

Young people who drink alcohol excessively are more likely to have higher levels of depression, anxiety and stress.

The ones who didn't talk about their problems reported more severe symptoms of distress.

(National Study of Youth Mental Health 2012)

LEARNING LOG

Bring in a piece of music, a picture or an item that represents relaxation for you.
Show it to your class and briefly explain to the class what it means to you and write about it below.

Review of Unit 2: *Dealing with Tough Times*

1 In this unit I learned about _____

_____

_____

2 I think that this will help me when _____

_____

_____

3 In this unit I liked _____

_____

_____

4 In this unit I did not like _____

_____

_____

5 I would like to find out more about _____

_____

_____

6 This unit links with (name another unit in SPHE or another subject) _____

_____

_____

UNIT 3 Change and Loss

KEY WORDS

Change

Loss

Gain

Change and Loss

Our lives change all of the time. In the last year you have had some major changes in your life. You have left primary school and moved to post-primary school. That change alone meant that many of you moved to a new building, in a new area and you spend your days with new people, doing new activities.

Some people find change difficult, and it can be. Others see it as a challenge, and are full of excitement when anything changes. Most people are somewhere in the middle. They see that each change usually involves a **loss** and a **gain**. Sometime change is very tough and you can need help if you are to get through it safely and healthily.

If you look at the two diagrams below, Figure 1 and Figure 1A, you can see that a change in your life, like having to get the bus to your new school, can mean that you lose and gain something.

The loss in the example is having to get out of bed an hour earlier. Other losses could be not getting to pick what radio station you listen to in the car on the way to school or not being able to ask a parent for money for something you've forgotten.

The gain is the fun you will have on the bus. Other gains could be having space between home and school or getting to meet students from other schools on your way to and from school.

If you are wondering how to deal with this change look at the 'What Helps?' section of the triangle. 'Making friends with others on the bus' should help as it will make your bus journey something you look forward to. Listening to music on your phone can also help if you find the bus a bit overwhelming in the beginning. Getting everything organised before you go to bed can also help if time is tight in the morning.

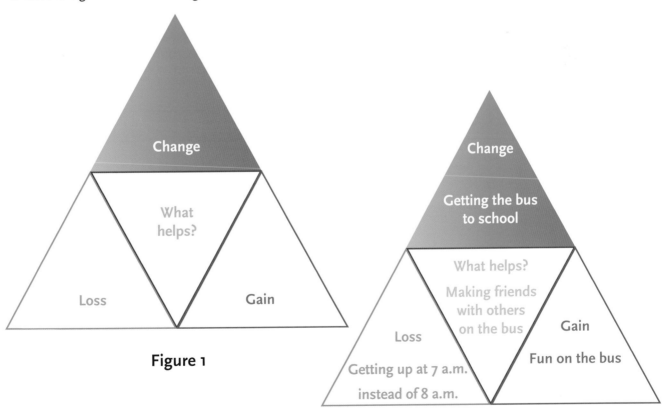

Figure 1

Figure 1A

1 Change: loss and gain in the last year

Note: Before you do this activity remember your Class Rules about sensitivity and kindness.

In groups of four, take a sheet of paper each and copy the Figure 1 triangle. Make sure you insert the headings in the four triangles and leave enough space to write new text below each one.

Each member of the group writes one change they experienced in the last twelve months. They then pass the sheets clockwise around the group. Each member fills in one loss they think could result from that change. The sheet is passed again and each member fills in one gain that could result from the change listed on their sheet.

Finally, each member fills in the 'What Helps?' section, listing something, or some person, they think would be helpful in making this change.

Now share the completed sheets with the group and answer the questions below.

1 Are all the changes relevant to all the people in your group?

_____

2 Are there any other losses or gains that might be included in each one?

_____

3 What other things could be included in the 'What Helps?' triangle?

_____

Now share what your group did with the other groups in your class.

Class question: Did any other group choose the same change to look at as your group? If yes, what can you learn from how they looked at that particular change?

_____

_____

Using what you have learned in this lesson, make a short video clip for students who are the same age as you on how to manage change in their lives. Save your video in your e-folder.

LEARNING LOG

Tips for managing change

- Don't let your imagination run wild. Ask yourself, 'What's the worst that can happen?' Usually it's not as bad as you feared.

- Can you control it? Check if there is anything you can do to lessen the impact of the change. Then do it!

- Look at the good side or gain to be made from the change. As we have seen, most change has a good side. Focus on this. For example, changing schools and moving to a post-primary school might allow you to try new subjects such as wood materials technology, classical studies or Spanish, or to learn more about subjects you are already interested in, such as science.

- Keep yourself healthy. It's easier to deal with everything if you are sleeping and eating well and getting exercise.

- Get help – you are not alone. Check out the help agencies and websites below.

Useful Websites

www.barnardos.ie/teenhelp – a website where teens can go to for help and advice, as part of Barnardos' mission to make Ireland a better place to be a child

www.yourmentalhealth.ie – aims to improve awareness and understanding of mental health in Ireland

www.yourmentalhealthireland.ie – a national voluntary organisation which aims to promote mental health and support persons with a mental illness

www.reachout.com – a support service for young people going through a tough time with information on the issues that matter to young people, signposts to other services and the opportunity to join a supportive online mental health community

Review of Unit 3: *Change and Loss*

1. In this unit I learned about _____

_____

_____

2. I think that this will help me when _____

_____

_____

3. In this unit I liked _____

_____

_____

4. In this unit I did not like _____

_____

_____

5. I would like to find out more about _____

_____

_____

6. This unit links with (name another unit in SPHE or another subject) _____

_____

_____